Capital and Finance

This book applies finance to the field of capital theory. While financial economics is a well-established field of study, the specific application of finance to capital theory remains unexplored. It is the first book to comprehensively study this financial application, which also includes modern financial tools such as Economic Value Added (EVA®).

A financial application to the problem of the average period of production includes two discussions that unfold naturally from this application. The first one relates to the dual meaning of capital, one as a monetary fund and the other one as physical (capital) goods. The second concerns its implications for business-cycle theories. This second topic (1) provides a solid financial microeconomic foundation for business cycles and, also (2) makes it easy to compare different business-cycle theories across the average period of production dimension. By clarifying the obscure concept of average period of production, the authors make it easier to analyze the similarities with and differences from other business-cycle theories.

By connecting finance with capital theory, they provide a new point of view and analysis of the long-standing problems in capital theory as well as other related topics such as the use of neoclassical production functions and theorizing about business cycles. Finally, they emphasize that the relevance of their application rests on both its policy implications and its contributions to contemporary economic theory.

Peter Lewin is Professor of economics in the Naveen Jindal School of Management at the University of Texas at Dallas.

Nicolás Cachanosky is Associate Professor of economics at the Metropolitan State University of Denver.

Routledge International Studies in Money and Banking

Financial Markets of the Arab Gulf
Power, Politics and Money
Jean-François Seznec and Samer Mosis

Performance Measurement Systems in Banks
Rahat Munir and Kevin Baird

Financial Literacy in Europe
Assessment Methodologies and Evidence from European Countries
Gianni Nicolini

Money, Inflation and Business Cycles
The Cantillon Effect and the Economy
Arkadiusz Sieroń

Public Value Theory and Budgeting
International Perspectives
Usman W. Chohan

Venture Capital Performance
A Comparative Study of Investment Practices in Europe and the USA
Keith Arundale

Complexities of Financial Globalisation
Analytical and Policy Issues in Emerging and Developing Economies
Tony Cavoli, Sasidaran Gopalan and Ramkishen S. Rajan

Capital and Finance
Theory and History
Peter Lewin and Nicolás Cachanosky

For more information about this series, please visit:
https://www.routledge.com/Routledge-International-Studies-in-Money-and-Banking/book-series/SE0403

Capital and Finance

Theory and History

Peter Lewin and
Nicolás Cachanosky

Routledge
Taylor & Francis Group
LONDON AND NEW YORK

First published 2021
by Routledge
2 Park Square, Milton Park, Abingdon, Oxon OX14 4RN

and by Routledge
52 Vanderbilt Avenue, New York, NY 10017

Routledge is an imprint of the Taylor & Francis Group, an informa business

British Library Cataloguing-in-Publication Data
A catalogue record for this book is available from the British Library

Library of Congress Cataloging-in-Publication Data
Names: Lewin, Peter, 1948– author. | Cachanosky, Nicolás, 1981– author.
Title: Capital and finance : theory and history / Peter Lewin
and Nicolás Cachanosky.
Description: 1 Edition. | New York : Routledge, 2020. |
Series: Routledge international studies in money and banking |
Includes bibliographical references and index.
Identifiers: LCCN 2020007919 (print) | LCCN 2020007920 (ebook) |
ISBN 9780367143725 (hardback) | ISBN 9780429031687 (ebook)
Subjects: LCSH: Capital. | Finance. | Economic value added. | Business cycles.
Classification: LCC HB501 .L49 2020 (print) |
LCC HB501 (ebook) | DDC 332/.041–dc23
LC record available at https://lccn.loc.gov/2020007919
LC ebook record available at https://lccn.loc.gov/2020007920

ISBN: 978-0-367-14372-5 (hbk)
ISBN: 978-0-429-03168-7 (ebk)

Typeset in Times New Roman
by Newgen Publishing UK

Contents

Figures

Tables

Preface

This book is the product of many years of thinking and writing about a new approach to capital theory in economics. Lewin's previous work on Austrian capital theory (culminating in Lewin, 1999) was the reason Cachanosky sent him a paper purporting to provide a new measure of Böhm-Bawerk's average period of production (APP) that avoided all of the previous difficulties and controversies that surround that concept. An initially skeptical Lewin became a willing and enthusiastic co-author of that paper (Cachanosky & Lewin, 2014) and many others to follow on the far-reaching implications of this new perspective.

In the course of this work we discovered, surprisingly, that John Hicks had already in 1939, in his seminal work *Value and Capital*, provided a clear exposition of this approach to the average period of production, which he called the average period (AP). Hicks explicitly suggested that it was a viable and preferable alternative to the Böhm-Bawerkian approach. (This concept had been independently discovered by Frederik Macaulay in 1938 which he called "duration," the name by which it is known today.) In addition, Hicks pointed out significantly that the AP was *also* a measure of the interest elasticity of the value of the production project with respect to the discount factor, (which directly reflects the proportional sensitivity of the project's value with respect to change in the discount rate) something that was a vitally important ingredient of the then-developing Austrian business-cycle theory (ABCT). Astoundingly, this contribution seems to have had no influence on the large volume of work on ABCT (or on Austrian capital theory) in the period that followed.

Once we realized this, and the implication that much of the controversy surrounding capital theory and the business cycle might have been avoided if duration had been incorporated into the discussion, we attempted to spell it all out – both the history-of-thought implications and the various applications to economic theory and current policy concerns that we discovered. This book is an attempt to bring it all together in a comprehensive account. Accordingly, we acknowledge our debt to our previous work and publishers, citations to which appear throughout. Part II, in particular, makes use of insights laid out in Lewin and Cachanosky (2019), which has been suitably adapted and extended here.

We are indebted to too many people to name who have, over the years, in discussion, and in reading our work, provided feedback. We single out Roger Koppl who, many years ago, first suggested to each of us separately, that the concept of duration was worthy of attention for its implications for capital theory; Steve Horwitz for his willingness to discuss and provide feedback on our work; and Lawrence H. White for his insightful comments on Hayek's thoughts on capital theory.

Lewin would like to thank his wife Beverley, his partner in all life's endeavors. Cachanosky would like to thank his wife, Nina, for her constant support.

Introduction

Capital Theory was once an important part of the education of an economist. For some time now, however, what is considered important regarding capital is thought to be contained in the theory of growth, captured in the neoclassical production function. Capital accumulation is seen to be an indispensable requirement for economic growth along with other aspects of the production function.

It is the contention of this book that the eclipse of capital theory represents a significant loss of valuable knowledge, and that the production function is not only incomplete in its portrayal of the nature of capital and its connection to economic growth and development, but is, in fact, a fatally flawed concept. Indeed, this has been known for some time (see Fisher, 2005, Fisher & Monz, 1993). In spite of this, the production function continues to be an important part of the modern economist's arsenal.

Recently, skepticism has emerged from another direction, namely, from a reexamination of the meaning of the concept of "capital" itself (see Hodgson 2014, Braun et. al., 2016). Capital has proven to be a difficult and frequently confusing concept because it has three inseparable dimensions, namely, time, quantity (meaning physical dimensionality), and value. Economists have concentrated primarily on quantity, with the exception of the Austrian economists who concentrated on time. Value was always present, but tacitly implied, for example in the aggregation of capital as an argument in the production function, being as Fisher has described it, "a quantity measured in value terms" (Fisher, 2005, p. 209). By contrast, conceptions of value used in the area of academic and practical finance have been based firmly in value. Capital is there understood "in monetary terms."

Indeed, economics students are explicitly taught that, whereas the commonsense, popular usage, of the term capital implies a sum of money, in economics it means a stock of physical production goods, tools, buildings, raw materials, etc. This is wrong, and unhelpful. Capital is neither simply money nor goods, and yet, in a sense, it is both. *Capital is a value, or a "valuation" that refers to the values of particular production services, (which are derived from the employment of physical and human productive resources), by a particular person, or set of persons, as of a particular point in time, but with reference to those services as yielded over a particular period of time. Capital-value is the present value of particular production resources employed in a particular production project or set of projects (for example a business firm).* Looked at in this way, one sees clearly how quantity, time, and value combine to constitute capital, expressible only in monetary terms.

In this book we aim to clear up much of the confusion surrounding the idea of capital by unifying the financial and economic approaches to capital, effectively bringing together the three dimensions in a clearer picture of how they are connected. To do this we begin our discussion of capital, in Part I, with the value dimension, and show how this is connected to the use of physical productive resources over time. The time dimension especially is made clear via the introduction of the financial concept of duration. Duration, which is a measure of the "money-value of the time" involved in any project, is central to our analysis.

To see how other approaches fit into our framework we offer, in Part II, a survey of the history of capital theory that focuses primarily on the contributions of the Austrian economists, beginning with Carl Menger, and ending with the contribution of the eclectic economist John Hicks. The Austrian theory of capital, though seldom studied any more, has been influential in the development of both growth theory and macroeconomics, in ways not always realized, that will be made clearer by our evaluative analysis.

Finally, in Part III, we turn to specific applications utilizing this integrated framework for capital. In these applications we make use of another financial tool, EVA (economic value added). This concept was developed in financial management and consulting contexts to facilitate judgments concerning the nature of expected (estimated) earnings. From capital theory (Hayek) we learn about the importance of "capital maintenance" – providing for the repair, maintenance, and replacement of productive resources over time. The EVA approach uses information (judgments) concerning that part of total estimated earnings necessary to invest for future profitability. What is left of the earnings flow may be considered pure economic value added. An EVA approach can use this information in various ways. We provide illustrations of this from both microeconomics and macroeconomics (business cycles) and also consider how this framework may be used to consider the role of institutions in adding value over time.

This book may be of use to a number of different possible audiences. Readers with a particular interest in Austrian economics, and, even more specifically, in capital theory, or Austrian business-cycle theory, will likely benefit equally from all three parts of the book. Economists and finance specialists less interested in the history of the subject wil l probably derive most benefit from Parts I and III while moving more quickly over Part II. We use no heavy mathematics, but some sections require more mathematics than others and some sections address topics more esoteric and less crucial than others. These sections may be omitted or skimmed without loss of a general understanding of the flow of reasoning.

Part I

Capital, production, and time

> Capital (I am not the first to discover) is a very large subject, with many aspects; wherever one starts, it is hard to bring more than a few of them into view. It is just as if one were making pictures of a building; though it is the same building, it looks quite different from different angles. As I now realize, I have been walking round my subject, taking different views of it.
>
> (Hicks, 1973a, p. v)

The difficulties attached to capital theory are related to the fact that capital has three "dimensions," namely, *value, quantity (physical goods and services)* and *time*. These interact in any decision involving the concept of capital. The history of capital theory has focused at different times on each of these three aspects of capital. At all times all three dimensions of capital are part of its nature, what changes is what is the focus of the foreground and what is operating implicitly or less-noticeably in the background.

In Part I we survey certain relevant aspects of capital theory combining the financial and economic approach to the subject that serves to seamlessly integrate all three dimensions of capital. This framework will be used throughout the book.

Chapter 1

Capital, income, and the time-value of money

Capital and income

Ideas matter

Our ideas define how we act and how we interpret and analyze the world. Action is defined by its purpose. The thought of *how* to go from here to our end (the purpose) is defined by our ideas. The nature of our thoughts greatly influences the acts we take and the outcomes that result. Moreover, the *ability* to think in a particular way may be crucial to the achievement of particular results. The ability to conceptualize in particular ways depends not only on our intelligence and our level of education. It depends also, crucially, on the institutional environment in which we think and act.

This is probably most clear in the case of thinking in order to *calculate*, that is, calculating in terms of some metric or set of metrics, calculating what the outcome of particular actions will or might be. Calculating implies the ability to *quantify and compare* in order to mentally (subjectively) weigh the alternative actions that one is able to take. Since possible outcomes from our course of action lie in the future, they are *expected* outcomes. Such expectations can vary across individuals. The expected outcomes that each individual foresees will be weighed and compared according to the individual's subjective preferences. This mental ability to perform these calculations, facilitated also by the legal and social environment in which we exist, is of monumental significance, and this is no more true than in the area of capital and finance, which is the subject of this book.

The ability to calculate *capital-values* is essential to the making of financial investment decisions, without which no modern economy could exist. Capital-value is the result of expectation and calculation, which is contingent on the *ideas* we have of what capital is and is not. We will see that the question of *what* capital is, is more important, and more elusive than is usually assumed in most formal treatments of the subject. In addition, the problem of properly defining capital has significant implications in economic theory.

Assets and liabilities, income, and expenditure

We shall use an understanding of capital that is consistent with the following definition by Ludwig von Mises:

> Capital is the sum of the money equivalent of all *assets* minus the sum of the money equivalent of all *liabilities* as dedicated at a definite date to the conduct of the operations of *a definite business unit*. It does not matter in what these assets may consist, whether they are pieces of land, buildings, equipment, tools, goods of any kind, and order, claims, receivables, cash, or whatever.
>
> (Mises, 1949, p. 262, italics added. See also Braun [2017], and Braun, Lewin, and Cachanosky [2016])

This definition uses familiar concepts of *accounting* and *finance* such as double-entry bookkeeping and, implicitly, the difference between *stocks*, and *flows*. Recorded transactions can be traced to their effects on accumulated values of the resources owned by the business firm (assets) and the sums owed by the firms that are payable in the future (liabilities). These accumulated values are *stocks*. The difference between the value of the assets and liabilities is the *equity*, sometimes referred to as capital, and what Mises is referring to in the quote above. The *equity* is measuring the value that belongs to the owners of the firm. However, and this is where Mises's approach may need some further explication, *capital* should be understood as a reference to the use of *any* means of production rather than to its ownership. The *ownership* of said means of production does not define the nature of their use. If the owner of a firm owns a tool and decides to sell it and then rent it back, such tool does not cease to be capital because there is a change in ownership. The expectation of the ability to continue using that tool in the earning of revenue will figure into the producer/entrepreneur's calculation of the profitability of the firm. The tool remains an *asset* used by the firm regardless of who the owner is or how the opportunity cost is recorded for accounting reasons. It is, rather, more accurate to think of capital as the value of all production goods in the control of a firm, rather than as the value of only those that it owns outright. *Equity* as commonly used is most often confined to those productive assets legally owned by the firm. But a "contract" (formal or implicit) for the services of assets rented contributes in the same way to expected revenue, though the reliability, or stability of those contracts will, of course, feature into the calculation of profitability, hence capital-value. This will become clearer as the discussion of capital moves forward, especially when we make use of the EVA framework in later chapters. The viability of the investment over time depends on (the value of) inflows being greater than outflows. Capital (net-assets) is the stock from which income flows: the purpose of capital is to yield income (Fisher, 1906).

To repeat, capital accounting uses the idea of capital that is a monetary-value and, in addition, is the logical counterpart of income. Capital is the source of all income in the sense that in conceiving of the value of all types of productive resources we are attributing (imputing) to those resources the ability, when combined in specific ways, to produce a flow of valuable services, which is income. If wherever there is income there is capital, then it follows that capital-value should include *all types* of productive resources (including labor, human capital, land, natural resources, etc.) There is no reason for categorically differentiating these different sources of income between capital and non-capital. As we shall see, human, and physical resources are treated differently for practical reasons, ownership of the former cannot be transferred. The services of human capital cannot be alienated from their source. Human capital cannot be bought – it can only be rented by paying a wage. This approach suggests that the capital of any organization, at any moment in time, is the money-value of all the productive resources (of whatever kind) employed by that organization. The income that emanates from its capital explains its value. Note that, in this conception, capital is attached to units of production (business firms, households, individuals, etc.) It follows that reference to constructs such as "the nation's capital" should be interpreted with care.

A crucial component in the analysis of capital is the role that time plays. It is not just that action taken at any point in time can affect outcomes at future points in time. Since income that emanates from capital is earned in the *future*, time, and capital are unavoidably and inextricably connected. A benchmark to use to evaluate a course of action is permanent (or sustainable) income. This is the level of income that can be maintained indefinitely with a given value of capital. The concept of permanent income requires maintaining the *value* of capital constant. This implies that the cost of maintaining or replacing production goods that need to be replaced after becoming worn-out or obsolete (whichever occurs first) is accounted for. More broadly, the income produced by capital needs to be compared to its *opportunity cost*, namely the next best alternative income stream available to the decision-maker, taking account of all depreciation and other relevant considerations (Coase, 1973). Data on opportunity cost, however, it is not always available. As is well known, accounting principles may follow legal definitions and requirements of ownership and depreciation rates, but they do not always match the economic logic of opportunity cost (the value of the next best opportunity for the employment of productive goods foregone). Coase (1973) shows that there

Table 1.1 Business balance sheet as of a particular date

Assets	*Liabilities*
Value of production goods	Accounts and notes payable
Inventory	Other
Cash	
Accounts receivable	
Other	
	Equity (net worth = capital-value of the business)

is no universally correct way to record the use of resources. Again, our ideas, and definitions shape how we see and evaluate the world.

Following Mises's approach, the value of equity is the residual after accounting for the total values of assets and liabilities at a particular point in time (Table 1.1). The purpose of the balance sheet is to estimate the value of the equity.

Values must be assigned to the components of the balance sheet (assets, liabilities, etc.) In particular, production goods must be valued somehow. Their value, as mentioned above, depends on the value of their output. Such output is possible by combining productive goods (including labor) in finite and particular ways. The value (market price) of these productive goods is the present value of their expected output. Other assets such as inventories or accounts receivable are easier to estimate.

Note, significantly, that the value of labor-services is not listed in the balance sheet. This is because, as mentioned earlier, labor cannot be owned, and therefore it can only be rented by paying wages. If the productivity of the firm's fixed capital is increased by its combination with labor (or any other production good rented), then the increase in productivity is by default attributed to the fixed capital. This is an example of how accounting conventions that follow the legal definition of "ownership" affect how changes in productivity are recorded and even understood. By convention, the balance sheet includes only those items *owned* by the firm and the value of the equity depends on productivity assigned to this type of asset.[1] In contrast, Irving Fisher (1906) provides a more comprehensive accounting technique in which the stock of all production goods (human, physical, etc.), owned, and rented, monetary and non-monetary, are included in both the capital (balance sheet) and income accounts.

1 In the U.S. there is an accounting convention whereby if you use what is called a capital or finance lease, you report the leased property on your balance sheet as if it were an asset you own. If you have an operating lease, you record it as a liability. The classification rules are complex and somewhat arbitrary.

We may wonder about the effect of excluding the value of resources expected to be available to the business to produce income attributed to it. As mentioned above, their value-contribution is reflected in the value of the owned resources with which they are expected to cooperate. To get the whole picture, one has to imagine the rented resources with which they will cooperate and the value that will be produced. Therefore, an entrepreneur appraising a particular business must endeavor to see more than is visible in the accountant's balance sheet, which reflects the values imputed to its items following accounting rules. Entrepreneurs needs to impute their own values to all of the resources they imagine to be available (owned or rented) to the business over time. The accounting balance sheet may be needed for legal and tax purposes. But, to economically assess a business opportunity, entrepreneurs need to build a "mental" alternative financial balance sheet, which will be contingent on their particular expectations. There are important differences between the accounting and financial balance sheet. In particular, the former shows results, but not the reasons for what he sees. Entrepreneurs need to go beyond the balance-sheet information and understand how the results were produced and build future scenarios of what may happen should they follow various scenarios.

An income statement offers a more detailed picture in terms of what is producing changes in the balance sheet. A simple example is depicted in Table 1.2. Logically, income flows from the firm's assets (hence the corporate finance practice of using the cash flow from assets (CFFA) approach).

A forward-looking (prospective) income statement to estimate future profits, provides a way to evaluate a business close to the usual method of discounting a free-cash flow (FCF) (more on this below). The balance sheet reflects the values imputed to the productive assets of the business, the present value of their expected flow of profits. The income statement reflects the value of the services in terms of their costs. But, the cost of rented assets is recorded in terms of the contractual rents to be paid. These contractual prices reflect

Table 1.2 Income statement

Revenue	
Sales	
Expenses	
Depreciation allowance	
Wages	Contractual payments
Equipment rental	
Occupancy rental	
Interest	
Profits = Revenue – Costs	

a "market assessment" of what a combination of these productive assets can produce. These market prices relieve entrepreneurs of forming their own estimate of the alternative money-value of these assets. At least, market prices provide a first guess that entrepreneurs may or may not then revise according to their own expectations. This is a significant benefit of operating within the institutions of private property, voluntary contracting, money, and capital accounting. For non-contractual services, such as those yielded by owned assets, the accountant, and the entrepreneur both need to provide their own estimate. A useful way to think about this it is as the cost of renting the asset to oneself – or as how much could be earned by renting to someone else (the opportunity cost).

Economic profit is the amount remaining from accounting profits *after* deducting these costs. The profit-earner is the residual claimant, and he bears the risk of all the earners in the business. The other income earners (i.e., employees, equipment suppliers, etc.) are contractually protected. The profit-earner thus has the greatest incentive to ensure the efficiency of the business. In a market economy, the residual claimant is the one seen as the owner of the business with the right to use and dispose of it. To be sure, the expected income of a business project is highly dependent on the entrepreneur's expectations. However, the income statement also provides an additional important objective measure, namely, the recorded historical profit, or loss of said business. This is a reason why launching a new product for the first time on the market is a more difficult task than making an innovation in an already well-established market. The former does not have a performance-related historical record to use as a starting point.

The market process relies upon the division of knowledge insofar as specific knowledge about local circumstances and tacit knowledge about how to perform many valuable business operations is dispersed among the many economic agents in the economy (Hayek, 1948, Chapter 4).[2] The complex interaction of a large number of economic agents, each acting for his, or her own particular advantage, is beneficial for society as a whole. Unknowingly, each individual is benefiting from the knowledge of *other* individuals by participating in the market.

The market process is the environment built and used by entrepreneurs to discover the errors (losses) and enjoy the benefits of their right decisions

2 There is an important point to make regarding Hayek's well-known paper. Hayek's argument is not that market prices are both, *necessary* and *sufficient* for the market to work properly. For Hayek, prices are a needed input of information, but they are not enough to take the market to equilibrium. Other factors, such as entrepreneurial learning is also needed. On misconceptions about Hayek's argument see Boettke and O'Donnell (2013).

(profits). This process produces a constant reshuffling of resources. In Kirzner's (2000) words, the entrepreneur is the driving force of the market. Capital accounting facilitates the making of decisions but, of course, does not guarantee the economic soundness of those decisions. Market valuation is a tool in an environment that allows us to make rational decisions – whether or not those decisions turn out to be correct will be determined by the passing of time. To emphasize, the economic calculation of profits and losses cannot happen *outside* the institutional framework of capital accounting and (free) market prices (we will return briefly to this point in a later chapter).

The time-value of money and the money-value of time

The time-value of money: investment decisions

The time-value of money (TVM) provides a framework, a set of tools, to take account of the fact that individuals do not value incomes received at different points in time equally. As is well known, individuals have (time) preferences regarding *when* they consume and thus *when* they receive any income. Specifically, individuals have a preference for receiving income (or for consuming products) sooner rather than later, other things constant. Because of time preference, future incomes need to be discounted in order to render them comparable to current income. An investment decision, involving future expected cash flows, can be modeled to yield a single capital-value (CV) in a familiar way (Equation 1.1):

$$CV = \frac{CF_1}{(1+d)} + \frac{CF_2}{(1+d)^2} + \cdots + \frac{CF_n}{(1+d)^n} = \sum_{t=1}^{n} \frac{CF_t}{(1+d)^t} = \sum_{t=1}^{n} f_t CF_t \qquad 1.1$$

Where CV is the present value of the investment, CF_t is the cash flow (positive or negative) in the period $t = 1,\ldots,n$ (where $n > 0$ is the time-horizon of the planning period), d is the discount rate applied to any future cash flow, and $f_t = 1/(1+d)^t$ is the discount factor.

Equation 1.1 expresses a relationship between time and value as perceived by human actors. There is a large number of potential unknowns but, typically, the equation can be used to estimate the common unobserved implicit discount rate used by individuals. Consider a simple case, such as that of a bullet-bond (capital is repaid in the last period) with a fixed coupon rate payment (Equation 1.2).

$$P=\frac{C}{(1+y)}+\frac{C}{(1+y)^2}+\cdots+\frac{C+FV}{(1+y)^n}=C\left[\sum_{t=1}^{n}\frac{1}{(1+y)^t}\right]+\frac{FV}{(1+y)^t} \qquad 1.2$$

Here, P is the observed market price of the bond, C is the fixed coupon payment of each period t, FV is the face-value (or nominal amount) of the bond to be paid back at its maturity. Finally, the unknown y is the yield-to-maturity (YTM) of the bond. Everything is known except y, which can be estimated as the value that "solves" this equation. The essential take-away (regardless of how simple or complex the bond or cash flow is), is that an investor acquiring this bond knows that each dollar of investment (P dollars) will be *marked up* by y-percent in each sub-period (see Osborne [2014]). This is the essence of what is known as the *time-value of money*.

It is customary to refer to YTM as the return on an investment *already* made (such as a purchased bond) and to the internal rate of return (IRR) as the return of a *prospective* investment not yet made. Besides these differences in use, YTM and IRR are calculated in a similar way. Given a spot value of the cash flow (the price of a bond or the required investment of a business project) which discount rate makes the present value of the expected cash flow equal to its given spot valuation? The IRR (or the YTM) can be compared to market rates or the investor's personal own opportunity cost to assess the economic profitability of the cash flow.[3] It is usual that, for pragmatic reasons, expositions of present-value cash flows are represented with a similar discount rate for all periods (a constant rate with respect to time). This, of course, does not have to be the case. A proper valuation of a cash flow would use the rate considered appropriate for each period (e.g., as interpolated at the corresponding rate from the proper yield curve). We can illustrate this as follows.

Consider the choice between \$1 today and \$1 promised one year from today. Because of time preference we expect that any economic agent will choose \$1 today over the *promise* of \$1 tomorrow. Theoretical discussion on the foundations of time preference can be lengthy and cumbersome.[4] However, it is enough here to point out that the preference of \$1 today over \$1 one year

3 It is well known that the LRR criterion is inferior to using the magnitude of NPV (net present-value) when deciding among exclusive investment projects and that there are instances when the two criteria give different rankings. Among available investments that cover the (the opportunity) cost of capital the investor should choose the one with the highest NPV at that cost. This does not affect our discussion.

4 See the discussion in Kirzner (2010).

from now is not only about *impatience*. It is also due to the *risk* that the $1 promise will not be honored for whatever reason. The more time between now and payment day, the more time available for things to go wrong. Two individuals looking at a payment one year from now will likely discount the payment at a different discount rate given their different degrees of impatience and risk aversions. There is a pure time-preference discount rate (or *originary* interest rate in Mises's terms) plus a *risk premium* in each interest rate.[5] The rate at which the particular individual will discount the promise of a dollar one year hence can be written as d_1. Consider now the case where the $1 payment will take place two years from now instead of one. The premium required to postpone the $1 payment one year may be 20-cents (d_1), and the premium to postpone a second year may be 30-cents (d_2).

Generalizing to the case with a payment in each of n periods, the cash flow can be as represented in Equation 1.3, which makes use of a term structure of n discount rates $(d_1, d_2, \ldots, d_n)$.

$$CV = \frac{CF_1}{1+d_1} + \frac{CF_2}{(1+d_1)(1+d_2)} + \cdots + \frac{CF_n}{(1+d_1)(1+d_2)\ldots(1+d_n)}$$

$$CV = \sum_{t=1}^{n}\left[\frac{CF_t}{\prod_{j=1}^{n}(1+d_j)}\right] \qquad 1.3$$

Equation 1.3 shows that there is an infinitely large number of combinations of values of d that would yield the same CV. We do not have direct access to the individuals' own, personal, time-preference structure. However, in a financial market the observed term structures of market interest rates (the yield curve) gives us an estimate of the time preference of the marginal traders and, as we know, in general it is not a flat line. The "typical" yield curve is upward sloping (even though on some occasions, usually associated with crisis, the slope may invert). In broad terms, short-term rate oscillations are associated with liquidity preferences and long-term interest rates are associated with investment decisions.

Equation 1.1 is more pragmatic than Equation 1.3. The former assumes that there is, in some sense, an *average* of all the different discount rates of each period. It is important to note that the assumption that $d = d_1 = \cdots = d_n$

5 This analysis has similarities to the typical consumer choice of a lottery where with probability p a person gets paid \$ x and probability $1-p$ he or she has to pay \$ q or keep a *certain* amount of money in his or her hand. Such individuals will compare the risk (i.e., standard deviation of the lottery payment) with their subjective risk aversion to decide if they should play the lottery or choose the certain payment.

is a matter of convenience when the term structure of the discount rates is not crucially relevant for the problem at hand. In this book, as in many financial treatments of cash flows, we make this assumption for pragmatic reasons, not as an implication that this is the normal case for discount rates. Of course, we acknowledge that changes in the term structure or yield curve can have effects on capital valuation. Yet, for most of our discussion we are setting this aside to focus on the more general problem of capital valuation.

To illustrate, consider an investment in a startup business with an initial outlay, followed by fluctuating earnings, and expenses. Perhaps the large initial outlay is expected to be followed by a few years of negative cash flows, after which positive cash flows will materialize for an extended period, say ten years. Maybe after this horizon of ten years a restructuring or revision of the business plan will be necessary, etc. The calculated rate of return for this venture will be very sensitive to the time-horizon assumed. To ask at what rate a dollar is "actually" growing within any sub-period of the chosen investment period is rather irrelevant metaphysics. What matters to the investor is the rate of return (or the net present value) over the chosen time-horizon.

Investment decisions and the money-value of time – the important concept of *duration*

Because of positive marginal time preference (including impatience and risk-uncertainty-aversion), investments will be made only if they promise to pay a premium. In a growing economy, this implies creating value. Limited resources are marshaled and combined in ways that promise to produce outcomes that consumers value enough to cover the opportunity cost of doing so. This transformation process is known as *production*, and the more value added the more productive this process is considered.

At least since Adam Smith, economists have considered this phenomenon to be at the heart of the creation of the wealth of nations. Some economists have paid more attention to the role that time plays in production than others. Notably, the Austrian School of Economics (founded by Carl Menger) is associated with an examination of the role of time in production, giving rise to a body of work known as Austrian capital theory (ACT) to be discussed further in Part II.[6]

6 Not only the "Austrians" have contributed key insights. Important names associated with capital theory are Carl Menger, Eugene von Böhm-Bawerk, William Stanly Jevons, Knut Wicksell, Frank Fetter, Ludwig von Mises, John Hicks, Friedrich Hayek, and Ludwig Lachmann, some of whose work will be discussed below. Of course, the designation "Austrian" in the context of economic theory refers these days to the school of thought rather than the country.

Böhm-Bawerk's work is one where the role of time more explicitly plays a central role in the process of production. Since production takes time, the relationship between time, and value must be considered. One aspect of this consideration is the difference in income earned at different points in time (e.g., one dollar now or one dollar one year from now) as discussed above. Yet, time also enters in another subtle, and related, way concerning the connection between value and production. All other things constant, if "more" time is to be taken to produce anything, there must be a corresponding reward. This comes in the form of a higher value product. In Böhm-Bawerk's terms, wisely chosen *roundabout* methods of production must be more productive.

While the intuition behind Böhm-Bawerk's *roundaboutness* is clear, such clarity vanishes as soon as one tries to define precisely what various related terms mean. Exactly what does it mean to take "more time" in a production process? How should time be measured? When should the count start and when should it end? We will see in more detail in Chapter 3 the complications that Böhm-Bawerk's treatment produced. For the moment, it is enough to point out that in order to simplify the matter and, arguably, offer an example as an illustration, Böhm-Bawerk suggested the concept of an "average period of production" (APP). APP is a conceptual measure of the average amount of time one has to wait for the completion of any product. A number of scholars picked up on Böhm-Bawerk's APP and made it the basis of severe and persistent criticism. Yet, the *concept* of APP refused to die. Over the decades, it has reappeared in various guises, explicitly or implicitly, in a series of "capital controversies" (Lewin & Cachanosky, 2018a, 2019).

Even though Böhm-Bawerk used a measure of APP that is admittedly very limited in its applicability to real-world processes, the essential idea is incredibly important and became a precursor of much work on the nature of production in the modern world. One of the most salient derivations is the role of monetary policy in business cycles. Ludwig von Mises and Friedrich Hayek saw in Böhm-Bawerk's treatment of time the seed of what came to be known as the Austrian business-cycle theory (ABCT) (further discussed in Chapter 4 and Chapter 10). In a nutshell, if changes in interest rate have an effect on the discount rates used by economic agents, then monetary policy will have an effect on the present-value evaluations of investment projects. Through this channel, monetary policy can have real effects, in a dysfunctional way, on the economy with the potential to produce a boom-bust cycle. Specifically, by reducing interest rates, investment projects that would take *too long* are encouraged at the expense of projects with a shorter APP. That an investment project is *too long* means that it cannot be sustained (it will turn out to have a negative NPV) at the equilibrium or natural rate of interest.

In some form or another, ABCT makes use of the idea implied by the APP. And, even though Böhm-Bawerk's particular treatment is ultimately impractical, the effect of discount rates on time invested remains. The fact that Böhm-Bawerk's example has serious limitations does not mean that the generic *concept* of APP shares those limitations. In particular, Hicks (1939, p. 186) pointed out as early as 1939 that a valid form of the APP *does* exist. He called it the *average period* (AP). Interestingly, Hicks's construction is the same construct as that developed independently by the financial actuary Macaulay (1938) that is today known as *duration* (or Macaulay *duration*). Duration (D) is most easily understood as the average amount of time for which one has to wait to receive $1 from any investment. Duration is a measure of the "length" of the project's cash flow. Specifically, D is defined as in Equation 1.4 (where the terms are as previously defined),

$$D = \sum_{t=1}^{n} \left[\frac{t \cdot (f_t CF_t)}{CV} \right] \quad 1.4$$

Note that D is a weighted average of the *time units* involved in the project, where the weights are the present values of each period's cash flow. D is the present value weighted amount of time involved in the investment. As such, it is a *money-value of time* measure. The logic is simple. The economic significance of the time involved in the investment, the amount of time for which one has to wait for payments to be made or received, is dependent on the *relative* size of payments involved in each of the periods involved.

To look at time in terms of simple calendar time $t = 1,\ldots,n$ is not very informative. The same calendar-length n can have a very different significance to the investor depending on whether the payments occur sooner or later and in what proportions. The *time-value* of the pattern of payments must be considered as well. *Ceteris paribus*, a longer average period (duration), should carry a higher markup.

The importance of the concept of duration for us is twofold. First, while it is true that financial scholars and investment advisors are quite familiar with the concept, because of its significance as a measure of interest-rate risk (to be discussed shortly below), economists are not equally familiar with it as a concept and with its policy implications. Secondly, both finance scholars and economists use the time-value of money and associated risk and uncertainty in considering the preference of investors. But, in addition to this, the investor will consider the pattern of returns over time. The investor will be influenced both by the rate of return and the duration (average waiting time) involved. In the next chapter we consider in more detail the importance of D as it relates to effects on CV when there is a change in the discount rate.

Chapter 2

Discount rates and time

Duration

Financial markets fulfill the vital task of facilitating the flow of productive resources from those who own those resources to those who can make best (better) use of them. In a well-oiled market economy this works automatically, but not seamlessly. Considerable judgment and understanding are needed to make this happen. Financial specialists profit from providing their judgment, which augments that of the investing entrepreneur asking for resources. Financial specialists and entrepreneurs are faced with the task of appraising the prospects of a wide variety of investments. Any investment has *multiple dimensions*, one of which is the size of the return promised, as discussed in the previous chapter. Also relevant are various kinds of risk, including interest-rate risk (from fluctuations in interest rates) and the risk of default or bankruptcy. We are concerned here mainly with interest-rate risk (default risk is also reflected as a premium in the interest-rate required).[1]

As discussed in the previous chapter, any given cash flow has an associated *duration* (D) which is a measure of the average life of said cash flow. As is well known, duration can also be interpreted as a measure of how sensitive the present value of a cash flow is to its discount rate. Estimations of duration provide information about the potential change in the market value of a bond or portfolio, but they can also be used to protect, through *immunization*, the value of the portfolio from changes in the interest rate.

It turns out then, as first indicated by Hicks (1939), that D is *also a measure of the elasticity of the (present) value of the project with respect to the discount factor* f_r. It measures how much the net present-value (CV) changes with small changes in the discount factor. Hicks (1939, p. 186) starting from a cash flow, then proceeds to apply the elasticity operator (Equations 2.1and 2.2).

1 We are much indebted in this chapter to the work of Michael Osbourne for leading us to a more profound understanding of the nature of the familiar TVM phenomenon and we make liberal use of his formulations in our discussion (Osbourne 2005, 2014; Osbourne and Davidson 2016).

$$CV = \sum_{t=1}^{n} \frac{CF_t}{(1+d)^t} = \sum_{t=1}^{T} f_t CF_t \tag{2.1}$$

We may calculate the *elasticity* of this CV with respect to the f_t as

$$\begin{aligned} E_{CV,f_t} &= \frac{E(CV)}{E(f_t)} = \frac{1}{CV}\left[1 f_1 CF_1 + 2 f_2 CF_2 + \dots + n f_T CF_T\right] \\ &= \sum_{t=1}^{n} \frac{t \cdot (f_t CF_t)}{CV} \end{aligned} \tag{2.2}$$

Where E is the elasticity (or *dlog*) operator. Equation 2.2 follows from the rule that the elasticity of a sum is the weighted average of the elasticity of its parts. In particular, there are two interpretations of this equation on which we should comment.

Consider first the direct interpretation of the elasticity operator. Equation 2.2 provides a measure of how sensitive the value of the project (investment) is to changes in the discount factor. As long as different cash flows have different values of *D*, then it follows that any movement in the discount rate will change the relative present values of different investment projects. This will be an important issue in monetary policy as it relates to business cycles (discussed in Part III). This means that changes in the discount rate will also affect how the capital structure (heterogeneous resource allocations) of a business project is composed.[2]

Consider now that Equation 2.2 is equivalent to the formula for duration, which was previously interpreted as the average life of a cash flow. It happens to be that *duration* serves the dual purpose of providing (a) a measure of average period (AP) or Böhm-Bawerk's *roundaboutness* and (b) a measure of the sensitivity of capital-value to changes in the discount rate (we will have a closer look at this issue in Part III when we introduce the EVA® framework into our analysis).

The uses and limitations of *D*

Modified duration and immunization

Building on Macaulay (1938), Redington (1952) sought to use D to find a way to *immunize* the value of a bond portfolio from interest-rate risk. Redington's

2 In the finance literature, the term "capital structure" signifies the debt-equity ratio. It is used here, as in capital-theory economics, to signify the structure of physical-capital projects.

modified duration (MD) is closely related to D. The calculation performed by the MD is a linear approximation of the sensitivity of the price of the bond to changes in the yield-to-maturity (y), or, in equilibrium, the discount rate. In particular, MD measures the percentage change in the price of a bond when y changes by one unit. MD is, then, the semi-elasticity of the bond price (P) with respect to y. The relation between D and MD is captured by Equation 2.3:[3]

$$MD = \frac{dlog(CV)}{dy} = -\frac{D}{1+y} \tag{2.3}$$

The main difference between D and MD is that the former is an *elasticity* measure while the latter is a *semi-elasticity*, both of the present value of a cash flow with respect to its discount rate. The essence of immunization consists in building a portfolio in such a way that the present value of and *duration* of the outlays equals the present value and *duration* of the inflows. Then, the effects of a change in the discount rate at the margin on the outlays and inflows cancel out. It is important to emphasize that MD, as a linear approximation, is intended to be used for changes at the margin, that is, small changes. Since changes in interest rates have an effect on the AP of the cash flow, and the AP of the cash flow has an effect on the present value of the cash flow, the relationship between the present value and the discount rate is not linear, but convex. Thus, the issue of convexity is important when dealing with larger (discrete) changes in the discount rate.

Convexity

Since duration measures the effect of a change in the discount factor on present value, and in turn present value is used to calculate duration, there are second (and higher) order effects. When precision is important, and a linear approximation is considered insufficient (for instance, when immunizing a wealthy portfolio), this second-order interaction effect must be taken into account. *Convexity* ($\check{C}$) is the name given to the measure of this second-order effect.

3 For any CV, $D = E_{CV,f_t} = \frac{E(CV)}{E(f_t)} = \frac{E(CV)}{-E(1+y)} = \frac{E(CV)}{-\frac{1}{1+y}\cdot\frac{dy}{y}} = -MD(1+y)$. In the case of analysis in continuous time, *duration* is equivalent to *Modified duration*.

We know that since $MD = -\frac{dln(P)}{dy} = -\frac{1}{P}\cdot\frac{dP}{dy}$, then $\frac{dP}{dy} = -MD \cdot P$; where P is the price (present value) of a bond's cash flow discounted at rate y. Then, convexity is defined as $\check{C} = \frac{1}{P}\cdot\frac{d^2P}{dy^2}$.

This means that a bond with a larger $\check{C}$ has a price that changes at a higher *rate* when there is a change in y, than a bond with a lower $\check{C}$. Convexity is important for portfolio management because two bonds with a similar MD can have a different $\check{C}$. For instance, a sinking fund bond with a shorter maturity can have the same MD as a zero-coupon bond with a longer maturity. The price of these two bonds will be affected differently by a change in the discount rate. Convexity provides a more accurate estimation of this effect than MD (for a more detailed discussion see Bierwag, Kaufman, & Toevs [1983]).[4]

The above discussion is presented in the context of a simple bond for, which barring default, the coupon payments are known in advance and the yield-to-maturity is calculated assuming the same discount rate for all periods. As these assumptions are relaxed, the number of unknowns starts to increase further complicating the analysis.

Too many unknowns?

In well arbitraged markets the term structure of interest rates (the yield curve) reflects the pattern of expectations of traders regarding future short-term rates (through preferences for liquidity, aversion to risk, etc.) Thus, for coupon bonds, the yield-to-maturity will equal the simple average of the (expected) one-period discount rates, or the holding-period yield, only if all the rates are equal (that is, only when the yield curve is flat). If the yield curve is not flat, then changes in the discount rate are not uniquely related to changes in the yield-to-maturity. Any given change in the pattern of discount rates is consistent with a variety of changes in the yield-to-maturity, and vice versa. Duration does not provide an accurate measure of the proportional change in bond prices for all changes in the pattern of relevant interest rates, which may produce different yields-to-maturity.

4 The matter is similar to the situation facing an economist trying to estimate the response of the amount demanded to a discrete change in price in a real-world setting. The elasticity of demand (estimated for example from a simple linear regression) is a rough linear approximation to the desired result. It is less accurate the greater the curvature of the demand curve.

The response in the literature is to consider how knowledge of changes to the term structure, may be obtained, and connected to changes in bond prices to provide better measures of duration. It is posited, for instance, that the pattern of interest rates is generated by an invariant stochastic process, so that "derivation of a correct duration measure requires knowledge of or assumptions about the actual stochastic process driving interest-rate changes" (Bierwag et al., 1983, p. 18). Under a variety of such assumptions different, more complicated, measures of duration have been developed (Bierwag et al., 1983, p. 18 Appendix).

The assumption of a stochastic process mechanically generating interest rates is likely to have very little appeal to those investigating macro and monetary policy. The pattern of interest rates in financial markets at any point in time is, in large part, a distillation of the subjective preferences and expectations of the many trading individuals in the market. The issue is that the role played by the *structure* of interest rates – as opposed to simply the *level* of interest rates – adds a significant degree of uncertainty to the reliability of predictions based on the idea of duration. How important this is in practice depends on the particularities of the circumstances and whether simple duration calculations are good enough or a more complex estimation is required.

Thus, even for a fixed coupon bond, where the coupon rate, face-value, and investment period is known, the effects of changes in the pattern of interest rates adds to the unknowns. In more general cases, for example where the future payments are not known, but must be estimated, these too must be added to the list of unknowns. Investments in business projects are of this variety. In these cases, the CF_t are not contractually fixed, but are dependent upon a variety of complex phenomena, including the productivity and effectiveness of the business organization in question and the future market for the goods and services being produced.

Finally, as discussed earlier, duration is crucially dependent on the time-horizon of the investor which will, in general, not be the same as the term to maturity of particular financial assets. Consideration of this has prompted the following "drastic" judgments from Bierwag et al. (1983).

> A risk measure unique to all securities and all investors may not exist. A security that appears riskless to an investor with an investment horizon equal to the security's duration would appear risky to investors with either longer or shorter horizons.
>
> (23)

It is unlikely that all or even most investors have single, well-defined investment horizons (ibid., 23).

And also,

> To the extent that investors have different planning horizons, this finding, casts doubt on the uniqueness of ... any risk measure of a security. (15)

We may thus ask, after considering the extent of what is not known, or possible to know, what is left of the idea of measuring and reacting to the relationship between time and value in investments? In what follows it will be suggested that, regardless of our ability to "objectively" measure this relationship, it cannot be denied that individual investors, at some level, must be conscious of it, that is, of the importance of time in their investments, and will react differently depending on the extent of the "time involved." What matters is their perception of the value of their investment, given their particular time-horizons, preferences, expectations, etc. and how these change with circumstances, including changes in interest rates. Furthermore, from the perspective of macroeconomic policy as compared with microeconomic investment calibration, what matters most is the ability to predict the qualitative or directional change in expected capital-values rather than their precise quantitative changes, and though the latter may be significantly affected by the presence of many unknowns, the former is much less likely to be.

Using polynomial roots

Mathematical complications soon appear as we move from assuming one discount rate for all periods to different discount rates per period. Practically speaking, these mathematical issues do not matter much. The basic "common sense" analysis of simpler cases usually suffices for most purposes. For some investment purposes, however, the accuracy of duration and the discount rates used is more important. In recent work, Osborne (2005, 2014) and Osborne and Davidson (2016) discuss the application of polynomial roots to this issue. Some implications of their work relate to our discussions in this book.

The bond price (P) of a known cash flow for n periods can be written as a polynomial of degree n (the term to maturity). Let fv_n be the future value in period n, then:

$$fv_n = p(1+d_1)(1+d_2)\ldots(1+d_n) \qquad 2.4$$

where d_i is the discount rate (interest rate) for period i. Assume now that $d = d_1 = \cdots = d_n$ and $n = 2$, then (Osborne, 2005, pp. 3–8):

$$fv_n = p(1+d)(1+d) = p(1+d)^2 \qquad 2.5$$

Looking for the yield-to-maturity of this cash flow is equivalent to looking for the roots of Equation 2.5. We know that the "markup" or accumulation rate *per* period is the geometric mean of the discount rate. If, for instance, \$1 invested at the beginning with $d_1 = 0.2$ and $d_2 = 0.25$, then after two periods we get \$1.50. The (geometric) average accumulation rate[5] from $(1+d)^2 = 1.5$ is $d = (1.5)^{1/2} - 1 = 0.2247$. There is a value of d such that $(1+d)^2 = (1+d_1)(1+d_2) = 1.5$. In fact, there are *two* values of d that satisfy this condition. A polynomial $(1+d)^n = (1+d_1)\ldots(1+d_n)$ has n roots.

In our two-period example, the two roots are 0.2247 and −0.2247. The existence of n roots in a polynomial of degree n is well known. It is the interpretation that matters. In the two-period example, the positive root $(d = 0.2247)$ is the only root that appears to have economic meaning and, therefore, the other one is routinely ignored. The intuition is clear. Someone investing \$1 today for two years understands that the amount received will be worth more than the \$1 today. The case of the second (negative) root where present consumption is foregone in exchange of less consumption in the future would not be an option. It would, simply, be better to postpone consumption by *hoarding* the \$1 and maintaining its value constant rather than reducing it at rate d.

For the purposes of borrowing and lending money (valuable things), the existence of multiple roots does not seem to be of major significance. Yet, Osborne (2005, 2014) and Osborne and Davidson (2016) claim that the other roots do provide insightful information.[6] To more clearly understand their claim we need to consider polynomials of higher order than two. Consider, again, Osborne's example, where in exchange of \$1 today you are promised \$1.6 in three years (Equation 2.6).

$$fv_3 = p(1+d)^3 = 1.6 \qquad 2.6$$

This is a polynomial of third degree $[p(1+d)^3 - fv_3 = 0]$ with three roots. The *orthodox* root is the positive roots presented by a typical financial calculator. The *unorthodox* roots are the other two usually discarded because

5 In general, $d = \left(\frac{1}{fv_n}\right)^{\frac{1}{n}} - 1$

6 This issue is also implicit in the famous debate in the economics literature between the two "Cambridges" about the meaning of capital.

they are not considered useful or do not have a proper economic meaning. For this equation, the *orthodox* root is $d_1 = 0.1696$, and the other two are $(d_2, d_3) = (-0.5848 - 1.012291i \; and -0.5848 + 1.012291i)$. As we can see, two out of three roots are not only negative, but they belong to the realm of imaginary numbers[7] (where $i = \sqrt{-1}$).

Even though imaginary numbers have a widespread use in other fields such as engineering or physics, their presence in economics is rare. As a matter of fact, roots can be real numbers, positive or negative, and complex numbers (the complex roots always come in conjugate pairs, so that when multiplied together they result in a real number). Yet, there will always be at least one real root (the orthodox root). Economists and others, who have known this, have suggested that the only economically meaningful roots are those that are real and positive.[8] Yet, Osborne claims this is a mistake. If all the roots are considered together, then they provide useful, and meaningful economic information. It happens to be that this information also relates to duration.

As discussed above duration is a linear approximation of change in the present value of a cash flow to a small change in the discount rate. This is a first-degree effect. Convexity takes into account a second-degree effect on the present value of a cash flow when there is a change in the discount rate. Osborne's claim is that all the roots taken together include all the information available for higher-order effects. In terms of a Taylor series, this would include all the terms in the expansion. This means that by taking the information included in all roots it is possible to get to the most precise estimation possible of duration. This is of importance for financial entities that prioritize a high precision in their immunization strategies.

Osborne shows that every polynomial has a dual equation, such that the typical representation of a cash flow can be written as in Equation 2.7.

$$CV = \sum_{t=1}^{n} \frac{CF_t}{(1+d)^t} = \frac{\sum_{t=1}^{n} CF_t}{1-(-1)^n \Pi_{t=1}^{n} d_t} \qquad 2.7$$

7 For a discussion on the mathematical characteristics and meaning of imaginary numbers see Osborne (2005, 2014).

8 Osborne quotes Kenneth Boulding (1936, p.440) as an example: "Now it is true that an equation of the nth degree has n roots of one sort or another, and that therefore the general equation for the definition of a rate of interest can also have n solutions, where n is the number of 'years' concerned. ... Nevertheless, in the type of payments series with which we are most likely to be concerned, it is extremely probable that all but one of these roots will be either negative or imaginary, in which case they will have no economic significance."

Where $d_1, d_2, \ldots, d_n$ are the n roots of the equation and that for most cases (patterns of cash flows) can be more simply written as in Equation 2.8.

$$CV = \sum_{t=1}^{n} \frac{CF_t}{(1+d)^t} = \frac{\sum_{t=1}^{n} CF_t}{1 + \Pi_{t=2}^{n} |d_t| d_1} \qquad 2.8$$

These equations tell us that the present value (CV) of a cash flow can be written in terms of its cash flows divided by (1+) the product of *all* the roots of the equation or by dividing the cash flows by (1+) the absolute value of the product of all of the unorthodox roots multiplied by the orthodox root. Besides its mathematical complexity (or maybe unfamiliarity), this result has an interesting interpretation.

> Every n^{th} degree TVM (time-value of money) equation solves for n interest rates. We select one of these interest rates. … the product of the $(n-1)$ non-selected interest rates solving the TVM equation enumerates the number of times the selected rate is applied to an invested dollar during the amortization of the equation's cash flows. This statement is true no matter which of the n interest rates solving the TVM equation is selected. If the rate selected is the orthodox rate (d_1), … as it is in financial practice, then *the product of the unorthodox interest rates enumerates the applications of the orthodox rate (d_1) to an invested dollar during amortization.*
>
> (Osborne 2014, pp. 20–21, italics added, and notation changed to ours).

Consider a positive (or negative) shift in the discount rate from d to d' such that $(1+d) = (1+d')(1+m)$, or $m = \frac{d-d'}{1+d'} = \frac{\Delta d}{1+d'}$. This means there will be n markups (m), one for each one of the n roots, $m_j = \frac{d_j - d'}{1+d'} = \frac{\Delta d_j}{1+d_j}$.

From this, Osborne (2014, pp. 85–86) shows that duration can be written as Equation 2.9.

$$D^* = \prod_{t=2}^{n} |m_t| \qquad 2.9$$

Different from D, D^* would be the precise measure of duration for any change in the (selected) discount rate by m_1. However, this expression is not well suited for practical use. It requires calculating the n roots of a potential long cash flow, some of which may be complex numbers. However, Osborne shows that there is an equivalent expression that does not face this constraint (Equation 2.10)

$$D^* = \sum_{t=1}^{n} t \cdot \left[\frac{f_t CF_t \cdot \sum_{j=0}^{t-1} [1+(1+m_1)]^j}{CV} \right] \qquad 2.10$$

This expression is very similar to that of duration, $D = \sum_{t=1}^{n} t \cdot \left(\frac{f_t CF_t}{CV} \right)$. The difference is that in D^*, each CF_t is marked up by $\sum_{j=0}^{t} [1+(1+m_1)]^j$. Only the real numbers are involved, so, while involving quite a lot of computations, Equation 2.10 is fairly tractable.

As an example, consider the case of $n = 4$ for D^* and D.

$$D^* = \frac{1}{CV} \cdot \{1 \cdot f_1 CF_1 + 2 \cdot f_2 CF_2 \cdot [1+(1+m_1)]^1 + 3 \cdot f_3 CF_3 \cdot [1+(1+m_1)]^2 + 4 \cdot f_4 CF_4 \cdot [1+(1+m_1)]^3\} \qquad 2.11$$

$$D = \frac{1}{CV} \cdot \{f_1 CF_1 \cdot 1 + f_2 CF_2 \cdot 2 + f_3 CF_3 \cdot 3 + f_4 CF_4 \cdot 4\} \qquad 2.12$$

According to Osborne, D^* yields a precise and accurate measure of the change in the bond price for any discrete change in the yield-to-maturity whereas all other measures are useful yet "just" approximations.

Summary conclusion

In this chapter we have introduced and examined the concept of duration, a concept familiar in the finance literature but all but unknown to economists, including the small group of economists working in the area of capital theory. Our examination reveals the usefulness of this concept in economics beyond its uses in finance. In particular duration nicely captures the idea of the amount of time involved in any investment as appraised from the view-point of the investor. It adds the time dimension to the value dimension in a way not obvious before. As such it directly addresses a prominent issue in the history of capital theory, namely the attempt to calibrate, even subjectively, the time dimension in any investment, like the APP. In a very real sense, it fills the gap that Böhm-Bawerk's flawed concept could not. We illustrate this more fully below.

In addition, duration as a measure of the average waiting period (AP), simultaneously measures the sensitivity of the (capital) value of the investment to changes in the discount rate. This is an important concept in a number of contexts including the Austrian business-cycle theory (ABCT). That theory can be shown to suffer from difficult internal contradictions, which this interpretation of duration avoids. We will examine this further in later chapters.

As a measure of interest-rate sensitivity, particularly in the context of immunization against interest-rate risk, if precision is important, one has to take account of second order (convexity) and higher-order effects, and also of other complications relating to what it is possible to know about any given investment. We presented a revealing TVM framework (thanks to the work of Michael Osbourne et. al.) in which it is shown that the roots of any TVM equation have the interpretation of being the multiple internal rates of return of the investment and the "non-orthodox" roots, in principle, contain very useful information if a precise measure of duration is required. Complications that attach to precise measurements of duration, though useful to know for an appreciation of the concept, are less relevant for the more qualitative investigations that will occupy us in the book.

Part II

History of capital theory

Capital theory is path dependent. That is to say, the state of the theory at any point in time has depended very much on the historical path of its development. In Part II we provide an overview of this development, paying particular attention to the historical roots of Austrian capital theory, which greatly influenced conceptions of capital in economics generally, including the concept of the neoclassical production function.

Though economists before him were aware of the role that time plays in production, notably Adam Smith, it was Carl Menger (1871) who captured this most clearly, if briefly, in his pioneering work. His close disciple Eugen von Böhm-Bawerk (1890) greatly expanded on this. Böhm-Bawerk's contributions to the field of capital and interest were many and important, but not without problems. Menger was critical of Böhm-Bawerk's attempt to capture the time dimension of capital in his famous average period of production (APP). This concept, though powerful and intuitive, and, indeed, very influential in subsequent theoretical developments, turns out to be at odds with Menger's vision of a dynamic innovative economy and ironically compatible with a static Ricardian view. Not surprisingly, this many-sided character of the APP has provoked substantial subsequent discussion and controversy.

In addition, a generation later, the Austrians, Ludwig von Mises, and Friedrich Hayek, especially Hayek, attempted to use Böhm-Bawerk's reasoning to expound on the causes and consequences of credit-induced business cycles in what came to be known as the Mises–Hayek Austrian business-cycle theory (ABCT). This theory, though also intuitive, and influential from time to time, suffered from the internal contradictions that plague Böhm-Bawerk's APP.

The main response to this from within the Austrian tradition was from Ludwig Lachmann, who constructed an approach to capital as a heterogeneous structure rather than a stock of homogeneous productive resources. He attempted to capture Böhm-Bawerk's idea of increasing roundaboutness in the form of increasing "complexity." Lachmann's approach, though adding rich informative detail to the productive processes of a market economy, meant abandoning the attempt to calibrate the "amount of time" involved in any production of investment project.

All the more surprising then, is that – almost unknown until recently – in 1939 John Hicks, who sympathized with Austrian concerns for all of his long career, had discovered a way to express Böhm-Bawerk's APP in terms devoid of these internal contradictions, as already discussed in the section entitled "Using polynomial roots," and discussed again in Chapter 8 in more detail. As we shall show in Part III, this rebuilt average period, in the form of duration (*D*), can be used to great effect to extend the insights available from capital theory. The survey in Part III will provide a conceptual backdrop for subsequent development, and for a comprehensive financial framework that integrates the theory of capital. Part II is a revision and extension of our work in Lewin and Cachanosky (2019).

Chapter 3

Menger and Böhm-Bawerk

Foundations of Austrian capital theory

Menger's theory of capital

Value is subjective, all the way down

Carl Menger may be unique in being credited as the founder of two distinct schools of thought in economics. He is well known as a cofounder – together with Leon Walras and William Stanley Jevons, of neoclassical economics, generally understood as the economics of the mainstream today. The key insight and distinguishing feature of neoclassical economics, and what separates it from the classical economics of the nineteenth century, is the insight that value is subjective. Prior to this subjectivist revolution, it was thought that value was inherent in things and that prices tended in the long run to gravitate toward these "natural values." The work of David Ricardo (1891) in particular advanced the idea that the value of any good or service could be traced to the quantity of labor involved in its production – an idea picked up by Karl Marx and used in his account of the exploitation of labor in capitalist economic systems. Menger and the other founders of neoclassical economics sought to disabuse us of that notion. As they explained, it was not the cost of production that determined the value of anything. Rather it was the value put upon something by consumers willing to trade for it that determined the cost (value) of the resources used to produce it. Value determines cost, not the other way around. This was a huge "paradigm shift."[1]

1 For an introductory discussion, see N. Cachanosky (2012). For a detailed exposition on the differences in marginal theory between Walras, Jevons, Menger, and Böhm-Bawerk and the history of the theory of value and prices, see J.C. Cachanosky (1994, 1995). Also see the discussion in Kirzner (1960, Chapter 7) and Mises (1933, Chapters 4–7). One of the main issues with the classical theory of price is that it was involved circular reasoning. Final prices were explained with the cost of production. However, the price of production goods was explained using the price of final goods. As noted in this endnote reference, letters from Adam Smith show that this was a known problem, even though classical attempts to solve this issue were unsuccessful. By including the role of the *entrepreneur* and expected final prices, Jean-Baptiste Say may have been the classical economist who came closest to solving this issue.

The other school of thought Menger is associated with is the Austrian school. While there are a number of subtle differences between the Austrian school and neoclassical economics, a distinctive feature is the extent to which subjectivism' features in economic theory.[2] This is important because subjectivism in capital theory will play a central role in our exposition. The Austrian School is also known for its work in capital theory and its subsequent application to business cycles in what came to be known as the Austrian theory of the business cycle (ABCT).

It is important to distinguish between price (objective) and value (subjective). The price paid for any good represents an amount that is valued by the purchaser at least as much as the opportunity cost of acquiring the said good. The price paid for a good depends, of course, on the *marginal utility expected* by the consumer, an expectation that at a later day may or may not be fulfilled (such as buying a movie ticket to later be disappointed in the cinema). The difference between the price paid and the (expected) utility is the *ex-ante* surplus. Once the good is consumed, the consumer knows *ex-post* if his or her surplus was as expected. It is only at the margin that the price paid coincides with the expected utility of the good. This is why the price paid for anything in the market accurately reflects the marginal valuation of consumers. And this is the sense in which Mises (1949, Chapter XV.4) talks about "consumer sovereignty." In the end, resource allocation can be traced back to consumer preferences. The same principle applies to all economic decisions in all contexts, such as consumption, production, investment, etc. While the idea of marginal utility preceded Walras, Jevons, and Menger, these three are recognized as being the pioneers in incorporating this principle into economic theory, thus solving the logical problem that exists in price determination.

Carl Menger was the most thoroughgoing subjectivist of the three marginalist revolutionaries, and he endeavored to distance his views from the formal analysis of Walras in particular (Jaffé, 1976). Menger's work and the work of his immediate intellectual descendants at the University of Vienna, Eugen von Böhm-Bawerk, and Friedrich von Wieser, became well known internationally. Böhm-Bawerk's work on capital and interest in particular was considered a seminal contribution and it became known as the Austrian Capital Theory (ACT).[3] The essentials of this theory were used by Mises (1912) in his widely read work on money and credit, and subsequently by Hayek (1931, 1933, 1984) in his debate with John M. Keynes over the nature and origins of business cycles. By the 1930s it had become clear that Menger's

2 For a review of the Austrian school see Boettke (1998, 2002), Boettke, Coyne, and Newmann (2016), J.C. Cachanosky (1984) and Mises (1969).

3 Böhm-Bawerk (1896) is also recognized for offering one of the most consistent criticisms of Karl Marx.

approach had developed into one that was different enough from the way in which neoclassical economics was developing, to therefore consider it a separate school of economic thought: The Austrian School of Economics. Our interest in this work focuses primarily on a financial application to ACT and some of its implication to the ABCT. This is not to say that there are no implications for other branches of economics. Rather, it is to recognize the distinctive role that that this school of thought plays in capital theory and finance. It also serves to emphasize the role of *subjectivism* in valuing capital.

Menger (1871) distinguishes between two types of goods: *free goods* and *economic goods*. Free goods are those for which at a zero price, a lesser quantity would be demanded than is available (there is no scarcity). By contrast, economic goods are those for which, at a zero price, more is demanded than is available. Economics goods are scarce, have value, and have a market price if freely traded. Economic goods have value because they yield a desirable service to the consumer. A hammer, for instance, can be used by one individual to put a nail on a wall and by another individual as a piece of art hanging from a nail on the wall. The value of this hammer is subjective for each one of these two different individuals. The value of a hammer exists in the mind of the individual, not in its objective physical qualities.

In turn, economic goods can be divided into two types. Final goods or first-order goods yield utility directly. Goods that provide utility indirectly are production goods or higher-order goods. Production goods provide services that are used in the production of other production goods successively in a supply chain, leading to the emergence of consumer goods that provide services yielding utility. Thus, the value of all goods derives ultimately from the utility of the services of consumer goods. Israel Kirzner has called this "Menger's Law."[4] The value of higher-order goods must be *imputed* from the value of what they produce. This has been referred to in the literature as the *imputation problem*.

The distinction between stocks and flows is fundamental and important and often neglected. People do not desire goods "in themselves"; they desire what flows from having or renting them. It is the services of goods that are the ultimate objective of economic action. And, as Menger points out, these can be obtained directly from nature, or indirectly by production using produced instruments of production, i.e., production goods.

Production takes time

According to Menger, higher-order goods are sequentially transformed until they emerge as consumption goods. As civilization develops, individuals

4 Personal communication.

move from consuming first- (final-)order goods to using higher-order goods to produce more final goods than the ones freely offered by nature (Menger, 1871, p. 75). Production, however, takes time.

> The transformation of goods of higher order into goods of lower order takes place, as does every other process of change, in time. The times at which men will obtain command of goods of first order from the goods of higher order in their present possession will be more distant the higher the order of these goods.
>
> (Menger, 1871, p. 152)

If production takes time and also requires the appropriate use of higher-order goods, then it follows that there is a *structure of production*. Some production services must be used sooner than others, and some production services must be used together as complementary inputs. Some production configurations will be considered more "efficient" than others in terms of the value of the outputs produced. And, because production takes time, and because time is also valuable, the "longer" the process of production (the more time it takes), the more productive the *structure of production* must be in order to be economically justifiable.

> [B]y making progress in the employment of goods of higher orders for the satisfaction of their needs, economizing men can most assuredly increase the consumption goods available to them accordingly – but *only on condition that they lengthen the periods of time over which their activity is to extend* in the same degree that they progress to goods of higher order.
>
> (Menger, 1871, p. 153, italics added)

Economic development is characterized by a "lengthening" of production processes. There is an accumulation of sophisticated combinations of production goods and their development. People learn to do things more efficiently by using increasingly specialized production goods. As the *structure of production* is developed to new levels, total factor productivity (technology) increases. At any point in time, however, the knowledge of future events is incomplete and therefore there is uncertainty about the value of each production process. What *ex-ante* looks like a promising project, can be shown *ex-post* to have been an unsound economic decision.

If for Smith (1776, Chapter III, Book I) the degree of specialization (the division of labor) depends on the size of the market for final products, for Menger this also implies the lengthening (or complexity) of the structure of production. It too depends on the size of the market as indicated by the number of transactions it facilitates. This depends crucially on the presence

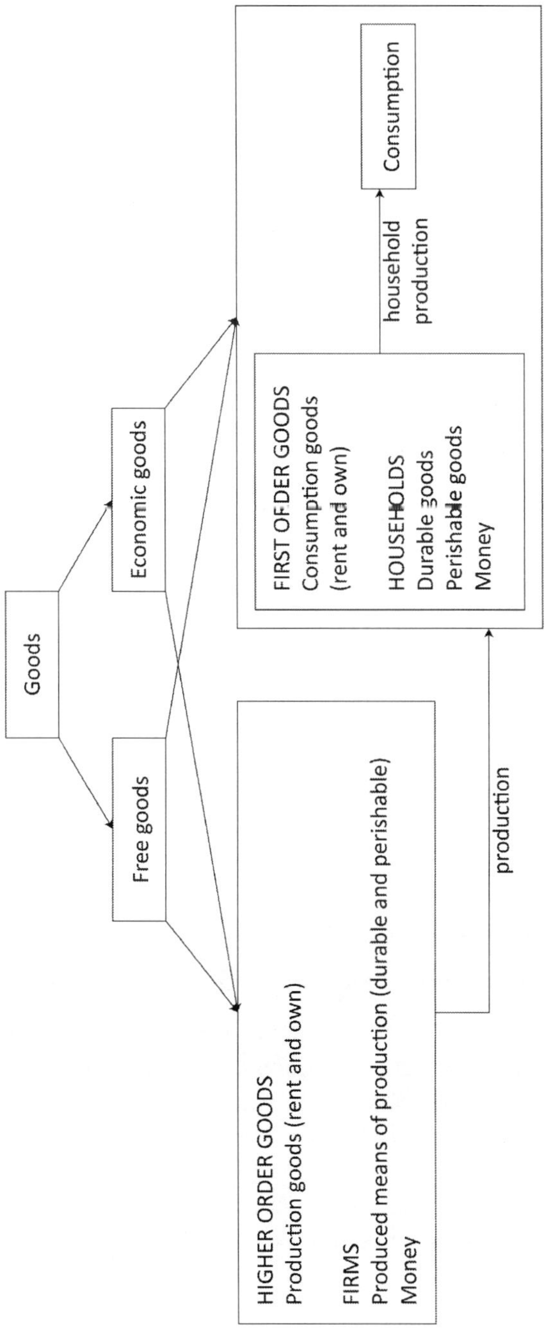

Figure 3.1 Menger's classification of goods and services.
Source: Lewin and Cachanosky (2019, p. 7).

of a medium of exchange, money. Menger (1871, Chapter VIII.1, 1892) offers a theory of the origin of money, where goods of high marketability spontaneously evolve into money.[5] The use of money multiplies exchange possibilities and allows for a more specialized and complex *structure of production*. In turn, money is also used to *measure* the value of production and exchange. Figure 3.1 depicts Menger's classification of goods including money.

Menger also points to the distinction between stocks and flows in relation to goods and services. The object of human action is not to acquire a good *per se*, but to acquire the utility flow it generates. All goods, final goods, and producer-goods produce directly, or indirectly a flow of services that is subjectively valued by different consumers. For example, when buying a house, the owner is purchasing a good that produces shelter services for a long period of time.

Menger's capital theory is consistent with his theory of subjective marginal utility. ACT is just the application of *subjective* value to the problem of capital valuation. Yet, this involves a number of issues that have influenced the development of capital theory in economics for years. One is the above-mentioned problem of imputation. If the value of final goods is what determines the value of producer-goods, how is this value of one final good imputed to multiple producer-goods? Another one is the role of time and value in the production process. A third one is the problem of capital heterogeneity, complementarity, and substitutability. Marginal utility helps to solve the first issue (which remains a matter of subjective estimation). Böhm-Bawerk played a central role in dealing with the second issue (in the next section in this chapter). While the third issue was a major concern for Ludwig Lachmann (Chapter 6).

Böhm-Bawerk's capital theory

Productivity, average period of production, and roundaboutness

Menger's insight implies that production takes time, and the more time taken in the production process the more productive such a process needs to be. There are two different variables, or dimensions, mixed up in this insight. One is time. The other one is the *complexity* of the structure of production. Böhm-Bawerk referred to this combination as the *roundaboutness* of the production process. More *roundabout* methods of production are chosen only if the extra time required is at least compensated for by their higher productivity.

The term *roundaboutness* is vague and, upon examination, turns out to be surrounded by obscurity and confusion. At first sight, more complex methods

5 Also see Mises's (1949, Chapter XVII.4) *regression theorem*.

of production are available to produce goods more quickly, taking less rather than more time. This is why they are *more* productive. However, this faster production process is possible only when specialized equipment is in place. *Then* it takes less time to produce goods (that is, after the new productive technology is installed). Time can be saved only after time is invested in developing the right tools. It is in this sense that Böhm-Bawerk considers more *roundabout* means of production to be more time-consuming. Somehow, more time is embedded in the production process. The present postponement of consumption is at least compensated for with more and/or better consumption goods at a future point in time. There is more time *embedded* in a highway that goes around the city than in a road that goes across the city. Once in place, the former allows one to go from one side to the other side of the city more quickly. For Böhm-Bawerk, more *roundabout* methods of production are also more productive. Furthermore, he conjectured that this increase in productivity was subject to diminishing marginal returns.

Böhm-Bawerk wrestled with the problem of clearly defining what it means for a production process to "take more time." How does one decide which project is longer: the one that is more capital intensive and produces goods more quickly, or the one that does not require so much time to set up but produces goods more slowly? To try to make the intuition behind this idea clear, he develops the concept of the *average period of production* (APP). Böhm-Bawerk's treatment, while trying to bring clarity to the obscure concept of *roundaboutness*, opened the door to criticism and the rejection of his approach. Nonetheless, as will become clear as we move forward, Böhm-Bawerk's treatment of the APP is quite close to the financial concept of *duration* discussed in Part I.

Böhm-Bawerk asks us to consider as an example of APP a labor-weighted average of time involved in a production process. His intention was, arguably, to offer a simple example to *illustrate* his idea. However, it was taken as a formal and strict definition of the APP. See the following example (also see Böhm-Bawerk, 1890, p. 87):

Table 3.1 shows a production process that takes ten periods to complete and the number of labor-hours required in each period (the first two columns).[6] Each period requires a number of labor-hours; at the end of the whole process, the final good is ready for consumption. The last column shows how to calculate Böhm-Bawerk's APP. In this particular case, the APP of the project equals 6.39 time periods.

6 In the table the period number refers to the beginning of the period, so we must put the total number of periods from the start to the finish, n, equal to 11. At the beginning of period 1 there is 1 period to go before period 2 starts and so on. If we had worked in continuous time, this adjustment would be unnecessary.

Table 3.1 Calculating Böhm-Bawerk's average period of production

1	*2*	*3*	*4*
Period #	*# Labor-hours applied*	*Production period*	*Weighted input*
t	l_t	$n-t$	$\frac{l_t}{\sum_{t=1}^{n} l_t} * (n-t)$
1	5	10	0.56
2	10	9	1.00
3	20	8	1.78
4	15	7	1.17
5	10	6	0.67
6	10	5	0.56
7	8	4	0.36
8	6	3	0.20
9	4	2	0.09
10	2	1	0.02
n=11			
Totals	$90 = \sum_{t=1}^{n} l_t$	55	$6.39 = \sum_{t=1}^{n} \left\{ \frac{l_t}{\sum_{t=1}^{n} l_t} * (n-t) \right\}$

Source: Lewin and Cachanosky (2019, p. 11).

Böhm-Bawerk's APP is shown in Equation 3.1. The amount of remaining time $(n-t)$ is weighted by the amount of labor in each period (l_t). APP is a labor-weighted average period of production.

$$APP = \sum_{t=1}^{n} \left[\underbrace{\frac{l_t}{\sum_{t=1}^{n} l_t}}_{weight} \cdot \underbrace{(n-t)}_{time} \right] \tag{3.1}$$

This construct of Böhm-Bawerk's contains a number of simplifications that could be considered problematic. To simplify, Böhm-Bawerk assumes that labor is the only production good needed. This neglects the use of natural resources. Furthermore, this approach requires assuming that labor is a homogeneous entity that can be measured and aggregated. This example also invites the interpretation that there is an amount of labor *embodied* in each final good that, somehow, has an effect on the final value of the said good (more on this later). Interestingly, in a particularly un-Austrian move, Böhm-Bawerk's approach does not include *value* and focuses on a homogeneous physical measure of hours of labor. The APP depends on an objective measure of hours of work rather than on its market value (there is no consideration of the market price of labor).

Böhm-Bawerk's illustration is designed to deal with the problem of what it means in a production process taking "more time." Which process is longer, one using two units of labor for three periods, or one using three units of labor for two periods? The labor-hour weighted calculation helps to rank these different specifications. Some periods contribute more to the production process than others. Those periods that involve more hours of labor are the ones that contribute more. Again, there is a close analogy to labor being embedded in the final product, and somehow in its market value. In the example used in Table 4.1 there are more labor-hours in the first periods of production. If the process were more labor intensive toward the later periods, the APP would be longer even if the total hours of work were to remain the same. However, the question of why the same amount of labor-hours at different points in time should have a different impact on the APP goes unanswered.

There is still another issue related to Böhm-Bawerk's treatment of APP. Böhm-Bawerk's presentation leads to the interpretation that the APP is a backward-looking measure, meaning that the question is *how long did it take* to produce a given good instead of being forward looking and asking, starting today, *how long will it take* to produce a given good. This became an important issue in the capital theory debates. For the APP to be measurable, the beginning, and end, of a given production process needs to be well defined. In the *backward-looking* approach, the end point (today) is well defined, but the starting point not so. This results in some paradoxical reasoning. If the ingredients of the APP are labor-hours, then there are two options regarding the starting point of a production process. Either we need to go back in time endlessly, to the moment when only labor was used as a production good before any tool was ever created, or to a starting point that is *arbitrarily* chosen. In the first case, APP becomes meaningless. In the second case, it loses its objectivity by becoming an arbitrary number. Frank Knight (1935) later argued that since, in a modern economy, production, and consumption occur simultaneously, the APP is effectively zero. Even though these are valid criticisms of Böhm-Bawerk's APP, it remains the fact that production takes time, and therefore it seems there should be something analogous to an average period of production. A faulty measure of APP does not make the concept of APP itself meaningless. It is plausible that, while he saw a valid intuition in APP, Böhm-Bawerk would not consider it possible to actually get a precise measure. He points to examples that, he argues, can be seen intuitively to have discernably different APPs (Böhm-Bawerk, 1890, Chapters 79–118).

Further issues: is Böhm-Bawerk's APP value free?

Consideration of Böhm-Bawerk's focus on labor-hours leads to paradoxical or contradictory results. According to his own argument, production processes with a larger APP would be chosen only if they were more productive. Namely, the rate of return should be higher than the opportunity cost of time (the interest rate). Even if not included in the formula, there is a clear connection to value. If the APP is going to be an explanation of the value of final goods, and in particular of interest rates, then it needs to be value free (it cannot contain that what it intends to explain). Yet, the way Böhm-Bawerk constricts his APP suggests that value is added *at each period.* It would be expected, in equilibrium, that each period adds as much value as the opportunity cost of the time involved. However, as Lutz (1967, pp. 20–21) shows, Böhm-Bawerk's treatment is either equivalent to a formulation with simple interest or is not-interest free. In either case, the APP cannot be used to explain the rate of interest (see the appendix for a mathematical treatment).[7]

Böhm-Bawerk's use of simple interest is a questionable *ad hoc* move. A compound interest rate is required for APP to make economic sense. However, this means that APP becomes a construct dependent on interest rates. Therefore, APP is not an independent measure of the value of time, which is in turn involved as the cost of opportunity of the time taken in the production process. Böhm-Bawerk's problem is to try to explain the interest rate *with* the APP.[8] However, this is not necessary or useful. The APP is important for other reasons. It captures the importance of time in the investment decision-making process, and accounts for the development of complex production structures.

Further issues: a Böhm-Bawerkian production function?

In the post-World War II period, attention drifted away from European-style economics (including Austrian economics) and capital theory, and a consideration of the importance of the role of time in the production process was also abandoned. The rise of Keynesian economics shifted attention toward

7 As mentioned above, Böhm-Bawerk's APP can be seen as a version of the modern financial construct, the Macaulay duration. Roundaboutness and the average period of production should be understood as the duration of the expected cash flow of an investment project (of which more below).

8 To be sure, in a static equilibrium simultaneous equation framework the interest rate could be determined simultaneously with the other endogenous variables, so that its presence in the APP may not be seen as a contradiction. But in the dynamic environment out of equilibrium this does not help. We usually consider the interest rate to be determined in the financial market by the demand and supply of loanable funds. In this way productivity, by influencing the demand for loanable funds, in turn influences the interest rate. But this is a process that takes place in real time.

the relationship between inflation and unemployment (the Phillips curve) and macroeconomic aggregates. For a "positivist" mind, these are variables easier to measure and grasp than the ambiguous terms of *roundaboutness* or APP. The role of time in the new economic approach became to discern time lapses between aggregates. A sub-branch of this new area of study is growth theory. The seminal articles of Solow (1956) and Swan (1956) triggered a still growing literature on the subject. The Solow-Swan model became the foundation of this field of study. The labor market was assumed to be in equilibrium, and therefore growth depended on accumulating more physical capital through investment (or in having a growing total factor productivity).

A typical neoclassical production function has three independent variables: technology, or total factor productivity, capital goods, and labor. A valued feature of the production function is its ability, using marginal analysis, to explain the distribution of output (income) between labor and capital. This approach was an important target of criticism for Marxist scholars. During the Cambridge controversy, Cambridge, England (neo-Ricardians, Marxists) criticized the neoclassical production function (Cambridge, Massachusetts) on the grounds that the concept of capital was ill-conceived beyond repair. If such were the case, then the marginal productivity theory of distribution would fail, and it should be replaced with a social-class based theory of production and income distribution. For Cambridge, England, the mathematical proof the neoclassical school is showing with respect to income distribution to capital and labor may be consistent, but is built on an invalid specification.

Interestingly, Böhm-Bawerk's framework has been seen by some as foundational for the neoclassical production function. Dorfman (1959a) is probably the most well-known case.[9] Let p denote the period of production of a stationary economy, N the labor force, and w the annual wage rate. Each period, the value of output for each period is Nwp. For any time interval dt, a total of $Nw \cdot dt$ value is added by labor. If labor produces goods at a constant rate, then goods that commenced t periods ago have incorporated a fraction t / p of the stock of capital. Then, the total value of labor embodied in the current existing capital stock is:

$$K = \int_0^p Nw \frac{t}{p} \cdot dt = \frac{Nwp}{2} \qquad 3.2$$

K can then be thought of as an argument in the function $Q = f(K, L)$.

9 See also Dorfman (1959b), Faber (1979), and Lewin (1999, pp. 73–92).

In this stationary economy, the labor-value embodied (or invested) in the existing capital stock is half the value invested by labor. As we will see in the next chapter, this coincides with one of the features of Hayek's capital theory in *Prices and Production* (Hayek, 1931), which in turn can be interpreted as a Böhm-Bawerkian approach to the APP. The ironic result is that Böhm-Bawerk's approach leads to a treatment more aligned with a labor-based or neo-Ricardian production function than a subjective Austrian treatment. Menger, for instance, raised concerns about this issue (Braun, 2015). Kirzner (2010, p. 137) reports that Schumpeter claimed that Menger has suggested that Böhm-Bawerk's theory was "one of the greatest errors ever committed."

Regardless of its shortcomings, Böhm-Bawerk's work was groundbreaking, and triggered vigorous responses. Related issues featured in the three famous "capital controversies," which occurred over five decades. In short, the first controversy involved Böhm-Bawerk and his critics, notably John B. Clark. The second controversy involved Hayek, his supporters, and critics, notably Frank H. Knight. The third debate is known as the Cambridge controversy (Cambridge, England versus Cambridge, Massachusetts).[10] As we have seen, Böhm-Bawerk's work transcended the Austrian camp and influenced neoclassical and Marxists (neo-Ricardians) as well. Directly or indirectly, a significant part of the literature on growth and production theory can be traced back to Böhm-Bawerk's influence, and before him to Menger.

Appendix

Böhm-Bawerk's APP with simple and compounding interest

Böhm-Bawerk assumes a *simple interest rate* (no compounding). Consider the following argument, which is a generalization of Lutz (1967, pp. 20–21). If simple interest at the rate of r per period augments the value of labor invested in the product, the APP can be written:

$$APP = \sum_{t=1}^{n} \left[\frac{l_t\left(1+(n-t)r\right)}{\sum_{t=1}^{n} l_t\left(1+(n-t)r\right)} \cdot (n-t) \right] \quad 3.3$$

We can use APP as follows to calculate the total interest added on the accumulated labor inputs:

10 For a review and discussion of the capital controversies see Cohen (2008, 2010), Cohen and Harcourt (2003), Kirzner (2010, Essay I), and Lewin and Cachanosky (2019, appendix).

$$\sum_{t=1}^{n}(l_t\left(1+(n-t)r\right)=\left(\sum_{t=1}^{n}l_t\right)\cdot(1+APP\cdot r) \qquad 3.4$$

In other words, the interest accumulated over the entire investment period can be calculated as the sum of the interest added to labor in *each* period, which is what is done in the expansion on the left-hand side of Equation 3.4, or, equivalently, since the APP (the *average* period of production) measures the time on average that each unit of labor is employed in the investment period. The interest accumulated can be calculated as the interest that would be earned by any one unit of labor during that average period multiplied by the number of labor units employed over the entire period. If we know on average how much a unit of labor earns during the investment period and we know how many units of labor in total are employed during that period, we can calculate the total interest earned. Therefore, the equation holds.

Now, solving for the APP, we can show that it does not depend on r. Simplifying Equation 3.4:

$$\left(\sum_{t=1}^{n}l_t\right)+\left(\sum_{t-1}^{n}l_t(n-t)r\right)=\left(\sum_{t=1}^{n}l_t\right)\cdot(1+APP\cdot r)$$

$$1+\frac{\left(\sum_{t-1}^{n}l_t(n-t)r\right)}{\left(\sum_{t=1}^{n}l_t\right)}=1+APP\cdot r \qquad 3.5$$

$$\frac{\left(\sum_{t-1}^{n}l_t(n-t)r\right)}{\left(\sum_{t=1}^{n}l_t\right)}=APP\cdot r$$

r cancels out from both sides of the equation, the result is Equation 3.1.

$$APP=\sum_{t=1}^{n}\left[\frac{l_t}{\sum_{t=1}^{n}l_t}\cdot(n-t)\right] \qquad 3.1$$

So, it appears that Böhm-Bawerk's APP does not contain the interest rate as long as only simple interest is considered. Alternatively, one can consider the APP thus calculated as an implicit value construct, with "value" measured by labor-hours. So, ironically, Böhm-Bawerk can be seen to have arrived (inadvertently) at a Ricardian "labor theory of value" construct.

If, instead, the inputs are seen to grow at a compound rate, then r will not cancel out in the expression, and the APP must contain the interest rate.

$$APP = \sum_{t=1}^{n}\left[\frac{l_t\left(1+r\right)^{(n-t)}}{\sum_{t=1}^{n} l_t\left(1+r\right)^{(n-t)}}\cdot\left(n-t\right)\right] \qquad 3.6$$

In fact, the APP with compound interest looks exactly like the formula for duration discussed in Part I, but for an historical process, looking *back* from the present and calculating present value, rather than looking *forward.* It turns out that the only defensible measure of "average time" is one based on accumulated value added, like duration, as we discussed earlier.[11]

11 The Böhm-Bawerk formulation in Equation 3.6 uses (labor) *inputs* to measure accumulated value, whereas Duration uses *outputs* (in the form of earnings), which is a crucial difference in a world in disequilibrium.

Chapter 4

Hayek's capital theory and Austrian business-cycle theory

Hayek's Austrian business-cycle theory

Hayek's triangle – a special case of Böhm-Bawerk's special case

The 1930s was the period of the emergence of Keynesian economics and its focus on macro-aggregates. The rise of macroeconomics in the 1930s was notable for its exclusion of microeconomic foundations. It was also a period of renewed attack on Austrian capital theory as inherited from Böhm-Bawerk. This was, in part, the result of the fact that the ambiguity and obscurity surrounding Böhm-Bawerk's exposition was aggravated by the model used in Hayek's *Prices and Production* (1931), a work designed to explain the deepening economic downturn that was developing at the time.

Hayek put a lot of emphasis on the structure of production as conceived in Böhm-Bawerk's framework. In order to explain the process of a credit-induced business cycle (as originally developed by Mises [1912]), Hayek borrows from Böhm-Bawerk, and constructs his own special case, making use of what is now referred as the Hayekian triangle (originally conceived by Jevons, 1871, Chapter VII). The work done by Mises and Hayek on this subject came to be known as the Mises–Hayek, or Austrian, business-cycle theory (ABCT). Hayek's (1931) treatment can be considered a special case of Böhm-Bawerk's already special case.

Similarly to Böhm-Bawerk, Hayek focuses on production over time. He considers a special case where the flow of inputs (exclusively units of homogeneous labor) is constant over time. If the same amount of labor-time, l_0, is applied in each period, then, from our discussion above of Böhm-Bawerk's APP, it follows[1] that $\sum_{t=1}^{n}(n-t)l_t = \frac{1}{2}n\cdot(n+1)l_0$, and since $\sum_{t=1}^{n} l_t = n\cdot l_0$, then

1 $APP = \frac{n}{2} + \frac{1}{2} \approx \frac{n}{2}$ (when n is large enough to ignore the $\frac{1}{2}$ or when the APP is expressed in continuous time and therefore is absent). Compare this with the similar idea offered by Dorfman in his version of Böhm-Bawerk's theory discussed above in the section containing Equation 3.2.

Table 4.1 Böhm-Bawerk's average period of production: Hayek's special case

1	*2*	*3*	*4*
Period	*Number of labor-hours applied*	*Production period*	*Weighted input*
t	l_t	$n-t$	$\frac{l_t}{\sum_{t=1}^{n} l_t} * (n-t)$
1	1	10	1.00
2	1	9	0.90
3	1	8	0.80
4	1	7	0.70
5	1	6	0.60
6	1	5	0.50
7	1	4	0.40
8	1	3	0.30
9	1	2	0.20
10	1	1	0.10
n	$10 = \sum_{t=1}^{n} l_t = nl_0$	$55 = \sum_{t=1}^{n}(n-t)$ $55 = \frac{1}{2}\, n \cdot (n+1)$ $55 = \frac{1}{2}\,(10 \cdot 11)$	$5.50 = \sum_{t=1}^{n}\left\{\frac{l_t}{\sum_{t=1}^{n} l_t} * (n-t)\right\}$ $5.50 = \left(\frac{1}{10}\right) * 55$

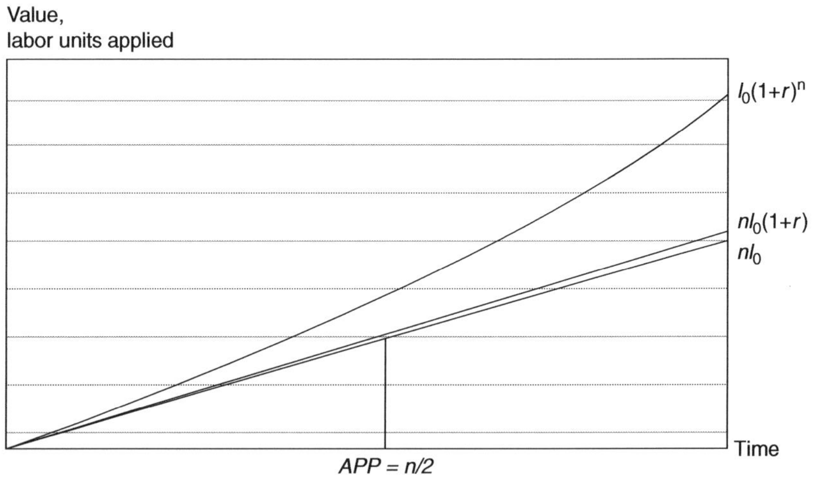

Figure 4.1 Hayek's triangle: simple and compounded interest rate.
Source: Lewin and Cachanosky (2019, p. 190).

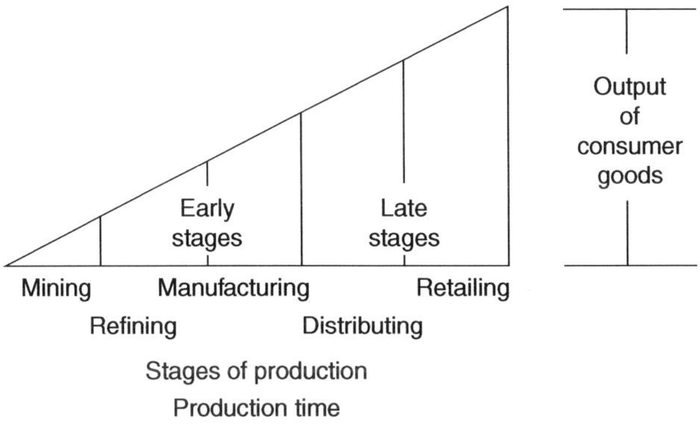

Figure 4.2 Hayekian triangle and stages of production.
Source: Garrison (2001, p. 47).

$APP \approx \frac{n}{2}$. In other words, and very intuitively, the APP in Hayek's special case is equal to one half of the total time taken from the first input to the emergence of the final output. This can be easily illustrated in Table 4.1.

In this simple case, each unit of input is "locked up" on average for (approximately) half the length of the production period. Hayek (1931, 1941) uses a triangle to represent the idea of roundaboutness where the APP is halfway along the base of a triangle as illustrated in Figure 4.2. The horizontal axis is a measure of labor-time. The assumption is that inputs are applied uniformly over time (column 2 in Table 4.1). If the inputs were not applied uniformly, then the graphical simplification would not work. It is the amount of labor-hours *and* how long they are "locked up" that constitutes the degree of roundaboutness or APP. With this graphical representation, Hayek attempted to capture the vision of Menger, Jevons, and Böhm-Bawerk (and, notably, Wicksell)[2] regarding the structure of production and to marry it to Mises's (1912) original ABCT exposition.

Following Böhm-Bawerk in assuming accumulation at a simple interest rate, the accumulated value of the labor-inputs rises at a constant rate and traces out a straight line above the accumulated inputs. The APP is (approximately) halfway along the time axis – i.e., at the mid-point – independent of the rate of interest. But, this is no longer true if interest is compounded, in which case the accumulated value rises exponentially and the APP is dependent on the size of the interest rate. If l_0 units of labor are applied in each period $t = 1 \ldots 10$, then the value of the unfinished product is augmented by the amount l_0 per period.

2 For a comprehensive overview of Wicksell's various contributions to capital theory see Uhr (1960, Chapter V).

If, however, a simple interest at a rate r per period is applied, then then final value $(t=10)$ becomes $nl_0(1+r)$. By contrast, if an interest rate is applied on earned interest (compounding), then the value in any period n becomes $nl_o(1+r)^n$.

Introducing stages of production

Hayek uses the triangle construct to highlight the notion of stages of production. He presents a simple sequential supply-chain model where each stage of production sells its output as input to the next stage of production until the consumption stage is reached at the end of the process. Some processes and activities precede others. Mining, for instance, precedes refining. Refining precedes manufacturing. In turn, manufacturing precedes distribution, from which retailing follows as the final stage before final consumption by the consumer (Figure 4.2). The height at the end of each stage shows the value added up to that point in the production process.

Hayek's triangle is an intuitive and useful expository device. It illustrates the argument that the degree of roundaboutness (i.e., number of stages of production) that can be sustained depends on the time preference of consumers. A fall in consumers' time preference at the margin (the reluctance to postpone consumption and increase savings) allows stages of production to be added thus increasing the accumulated value added at the end of the triangle. This is also an increase in the APP of the production process. In other words, the increase in savings allows a move toward a more "capital intensive" structure of production with a higher payoff at the end of the process. By the same token, a fall in the interest rate produced by consumers would send a false signal to producers who might try to add stages of production as a result. But their efforts would, in time, be unsustainable, because the necessary resources to sustain these new expanded ventures are not really available. Consumers have not reduced their demand for output to release resources for production at "farther away" stages of production. Consequently, the shift, and likely change in slope, of the diagonal of the triangle would be temporary, illustrating the boom of a cycle, while the bust would entail a reversal of the move. This is the essence of the ABCT as illustrated by Hayek's framework.

Note that introducing stages of production that capture the value added as production moves forward in time adds a value dimension to Böhm-Bawerk's quantity of labor treatment. What Hayek built is a constant cash flow with a simple rather than compounding discount rate. What Hayek presented is, in fact, the case of duration for this simple cash flow.[3]

3 For more detailed discussion on this issue and the discussion that follows see Cachanosky and Lewin (2018).

The simplifications introduced in Hayek's triangle in *Prices and Production*, after some initial accolades, produced a storm of criticisms. His model invited confusion and contributed to the rejection of Böhm-Bawerk's capital theory, which is also the distinctive component of the ABCT. Yet, many expositions of the ABCT still today refer to Hayek's (1931) model in *Prices and Production*.

Consider, for instance, the notion of "stage of production." The fact that a stage of production is an abstract tool (used to study capital theory) rather than an observable objective entity adds to doubts about Böhm-Bawerk's story of roundaboutness.[4] Note that the same reality can be represented by different stages of production depending on how the observer decides to "slice" reality. The number of stages of production can also vary. To define a Hayekian triangle requires a set of subjective assumptions about how to separate and delimit stages of production, given the available data. Once this is arbitrarily done, it is possible that one economic activity is present in more than one stage of production. For instance, the supply of energy, and financial services, are expected to be found along the whole triangle. There is also the phenomenon of "looping," where two stages of production provide inputs to each other. For instance, the energy sector sells its output to the financial sector, which sells its services to the energy sector. Stages can also move (to be sooner or later) in the production process during a business cycle. Another issue, raised by Luther and Cohen (2014), is that stages of production can grow not only vertically, but also horizontally. Hayek's triangle serves pedagogical purposes, but is ill-suited to guide empirical research.[5]

The legacy of Hayek's triangle

After the criticisms that his treatment in *Prices and Production* received, Hayek attempted to answer his critics and flesh out the capital theory underlying his approach to business cycles in numerous articles, finally culminating in his book *The Pure Theory of Capital* (1941). Against the backdrop

4 This is very clear from Hayek's later and final comprehensive work on capital-theory in which he routinely refers to stages by enclosing the word in quotes, as in "stages" (Hayek, 1941b, pp. 131–132, 140–142, 146–147).

5 The inspiration for much contemporary empirical research on the ABCT is Garrison's (2001) use of Hayek's triangle. This line of work investigates whether different industries (stages of production) behave as predicted by Garrison's model representation of the ABCT, where it is expected that early and later stages of production grow (vertically) with respect to mid-stages of production (Lester & Wolff, 2013; Luther & Cohen, 2014; Mulligan, 2002; Powell, 2002; Young, 2005). There are, however, a few exceptions (Cachanosky, 2014; Koppl, 2014; Young, 2012). These latter authors either look at an aggregate average period of production (roundaboutness) for the whole economy or the interest-rate sensitivity of different industries rather than looking at stages of production.

of World War II and the ascendancy of Keynesian economics, Hayek sought to solidify his contention that an inappropriately low central-bank-induced interest rate distorted the structure of production, and that the unemployment that ensued was a result of the unsustainable structure of heterogeneous capital goods that had been constructed. As Keynes had pointed out, in a monetary economy, individual acts of saving, and investment are separate and may be inconsistent. Yet, Keynes, and Hayek disagreed over the implications of this. For Keynes, this was a reason to doubt the stability of financial markets and the capacity of the market economy to self-correct. Hayek, by contrast, "knew" this to be false, and considered that the market had proven itself capable of handling an extraordinary variety of situations if left to its own devices.

Hayek's triangle, however, proved inadequate to defend this point of view. The triangle became a pedagogical medium to communicate his message, but the triangle itself *was not* the message. Hayek had hoped that the triangle, with all its simplifications, would serve the purpose of translating his message in an intuitive way. What was the essence of this message?

Hayek's general ideas were that unhampered interest-rate movements were necessary and sufficient to coordinate the plans of savers and investors. This coordination, however, was disrupted if the central bank engaged in credit expansion to reduce interest rates. As Hayek saw it, the implications of this are that credit-induced (as distinct from savings-induced) low interest rates provided a false signal that caused discoordination between savers and investors. Specifically, the low interest rates provided an incentive for reduced saving and increased investment with the gap being closed by an elastic money supply. Given the fall in saving, or by implication the increase in consumption, the amount of investment is insufficient to supply current consumption demands. Furthermore, it is not only that investment is insufficient as that is the *wrong kind* of investment, i.e., investment in production projects that are too "long" (too capital intensive). This line of argumentation required him to provide a firm understanding of how one determines the "length" of any investment project and how this related to the "amount" of capital invested in it. Furthermore, he needed to show that the lower the interest rate, the greater the APP, and capital intensity that would result from the investment decisions of entrepreneurs.[6]

To explain the business cycle by appealing to the nature of capital requires dealing with the problem of the *heterogeneity of capital goods*. This issue will

6 Recall that in the Austrian literature, the interest rate is the price of *time*, not of capital. Therefore, a policy induced reduction in the interest rate makes the price of time fall. Therefore, more time will be *used* in lengthening the production process.

be dealt with in more detail in the next chapter. Here we need to explain why this is so important for the ABCT. The heterogeneous nature of capital goods, particularly the fact that they cannot generally be substituted one for the other, but rather have specific, restricted uses, and must be assembled in complimentary combinations, implies that they cannot simply be reallocated to more sustainable projects once the current project is revealed to be unsustainable. Investments in capital-specific combinations are not reversible (it is costly to change the dimension – length – of Hayek's triangle). Once investment in specific capital goods has been made in an unsustainable, unprofitable venture, capital losses will occur, and the value of the specific goods involved will be revealed to be lower than previously thought. This constitutes the recession phase of the cycle. If heterogeneity and specificity were absent, investments could simply be undone and redone in a more profitable way, without much loss.

In using the Austrian theory of capital, and its particular formulation by Böhm-Bawerk, as the foundation for developing a theory of the business cycle, Hayek thus became committed to a particular framework *that relied on the absence of heterogeneity (or at least suppressed it) to illustrate the consequences of the fact of heterogeneity*. This resulted in the rejection of the ABCT for decades. His later examination of the complexities of capital shows that, even in equilibrium, it was impossible to attach an unambiguous meaning to the concept of "average period of production" or to show that such a quantity was monotonically related to the interest (discount) rate. While he was able to decisively confirm the importance of time for a thorough understanding of production decisions, and while he was able, under some restrictive assumptions, to give clear meaning to the notion of the multiple investment periods involved in any ongoing investment project – connecting inputs to outputs over time – he was forced to abandon the attempt to characterize investment projects in the form of a single magnitude like the APP.

> As at first contemplated, this study was intended as little more than a systematic exposition of what I imagined to be a fairly complete body of doctrine, which, in the course of years, had evolved from the foundations laid by Jevons, Böhm-Bawerk, and Wicksell. I had little idea ... that some of the simplifications employed by the earlier writers had such far-reaching consequences as to make their conceptual tools almost useless in the analysis of more complicated situations. The most important of these inappropriate simplifications ... was the attempt to introduce the time factor into the theory of capital in the form of one single relevant time interval – the "average period of production."
>
> (Hayek, 1941, pp. 3–4, see also 92–93)

Hayek's capital theory

Hayek and the average period of production

The first edition of Hayek's *Prices and Production* (1931) contains a simplified version of Böhm-Bawerk's approach as explained above. In a later work, Hayek (1941) attempts to provide a fully worked-out response to the critical reaction to the simplified exposition in *Prices and Production*. Much of the content in *The Pure Theory of Capital* had already been published in a series of articles by Hayek (discussed further below). The substance of the said articles ultimately came to be *The Pure Theory of Capital*. For various reasons, this book did not achieve its objective "to develop a capital theory that could be fully integrated into business-cycle theory" (White, 1941, pp. xviii–xiv). Rather, to this day, most of the work on ABCT relies directly or indirectly on *Prices and Production*, where the stages of production take center stage, rather than in *The Pure Theory of Capital*. Hayek was unsuccessful in clearing up capital-theory ambiguities that affected the evolution of ABCT for years to come.

Following Mises (1912), Hayek's work on capital theory was motivated by the intuitive claim that a credit expansion that sets the interest rate below its natural or equilibrium value encourages spending on relative "long-term" investment projects that are not sustainable. If this effect were to be strong enough and sustained for a certain period of time, it would ultimately produce market imbalances that, when corrected, would statistically look large enough to be observed as a business cycle. Hayek's claim seemed to be confirmed by a number of historical episodes. It was, also, a claim that Hayek said he "knew" to be correct but had yet, even after *The Pure Theory of Capital*, still to prove.[7] Hayek's work on capital theory consists of various attempts to find a suitable alternative to the APP that would allow him to support what he *knew* to be true about business cycles.

Hayek's quest on capital theory led him to consider other aspects such as the issues of capital consumption, capital maintenance, capital accumulation, economic growth, and related topics. Yet, the original impetus for his work appears to have been the criticisms of the APP, particularly by Frank Knight, with whom Hayek engaged in debate in the 1930s.[8] This debate is referred to as the second of the three "capital controversies."[9]

7 "I rather hoped that what I'd done in capital theory would be continued by others. [...] [Completing it myself] would have meant working for a result which I already knew, but I had to prove" (Hayek, 1994, p. 96). Also McClure, Spector, and Thomas (2018), from where this quote is reproduced), and Lewin (2018).

8 See Hayek (1934, 1935, 1936), Knight (1935) and Machlup (1935a, 1935b).

9 The first capital controversy refers to the debate between Böhm-Bawerk and his critics, notably J.B. Clark. This controversy in many ways foreshadowed the second one. Böhm-Bawerk's

Beyond the APP, to what?

The APP is a construct designed to summarize in one number the amount of time involved in any production process. After *Prices and Production* Hayek realized that this was a bad idea. Nevertheless, in a series of articles, among the most important of which are Hayek (1934, 1935, 1936, 1941), he strongly supported the important role of time in production and investment decisions. This also implies dealing with the role that capital and time play in the ABCT. Hayek tried to go beyond the simple Böhm-Bawerkian model found in *Prices and Production* by including durable capital goods and allowing for continuous input and output flows through time. Much of this work is performed in terms of static equilibrium analysis. Yet, in his verbal remarks we find many valuable insights applicable to a dynamic world of continual change.

Böhm-Bawerk's and Hayek's scheme can be viewed in two distinct ways. The first one is as a picture of the progress of a particular unit of input through time as it proceeds through the production process, accumulating value. The second one is as a snapshot of the various "stages of production" existing at a *single* point of time in an ongoing production process that produces output continuously. These two views look the same in a stationary world. Hayek (1934, 1941) expresses both views simultaneously by adding a time dimension. We are asked to try to follow the progress through time of the whole array of inputs existing at every point in time. Instead of characterizing the production process in a single period, Hayek identifies a function, "the time distribution of output due to a moment's input," which can be looked at in two ways, as an *input function* that shows the share of the total input of a particular date represented in each date's output, and as an *output function* showing the share of the total output over time of a single date's input represented in each date's output. The difference between the two functions in equilibrium represents the compound interest accrued and indicates the greater productivity of those processes that take "more time" (Hayek, 1934, 1941, Chapters 8–9, and the editor's introduction, p. xxiii).

Rather than referring to a single APP, Hayek uses multiple *production periods* or *investment periods*. Hayek also significantly recognizes that any metric of the amount of time involved in production cannot be independent

particular conception of production using the APP was seen by Clark, as by Knight, as overly simplified, contradictory, and unhelpful in understanding the role of capital in the economy. Both Clark and Knight preferred a timeless conception of capital and production, where, in equilibrium, production and consumption are seen to be simultaneous, and speculations about "production periods" are beside the point. While Hayek never even came close to accepting this static equilibrium framework, except as a preliminary theoretical exercise, he did accept the criticisms of the APP.

of the rate of interest: something already evident in the simple APP with compound interest. As soon as this is realized, the notion of a single, invariant period of production disappears,

> because the reinvestment of interest accrued up to any moment of time has to be counted as part of the total investment. It is for this reason ... that is impossible to substitute any one-dimensional magnitude like 'average period of production' for the concept of the investment function. For *there is no one single average period for which a quantity of factors could be invested with the result that the quantity of capital so created would be the same as if the same quantity of factors had been invested for the range of periods described by a given investment function, whatever the rate of interest. The mean value of those different investment periods which would satisfy this condition would have to be different for any rate of interest.*
>
> (Hayek, 1934, p. 217, italics added)

Nevertheless, Hayek still attempted to preserve what he knew was true, namely the implications of the ABCT that a fall in the money interest rate would lead on net, in equilibrium, to an increase in the number of "long" investment periods. He argued this in different ways, one of which is known as the Ricardo Effect. Hayek recognized that the input and output functions would not (in general) be invariant to changes in the interest rate. Rather, an interest-rate fall would cause a temporal reshuffling of inputs for the production of any set of outputs (which can also change) *making the investment of any input earlier in the process more profitable*. In the case in which the money interest-rate reduction was the result of money-credit expansion, and not an increase in savings, this reshuffling would prove to be largely unprofitable and unsustainable, producing the anatomy of the ABCT.[10]

The cases that Hayek investigates to motivate the idea that interest-rate decreases can be shown to shift resources to early stages of production, and other effects, depend crucially on the simplifying assumptions he makes. They are illustrations of what *might* happen (if conditional assumptions hold) rather than of what *must* happen. It depends mostly on the shape of the input and output flows that constitute the investment in a manner familiar now from the arithmetic of the present value of cash flows in the financial literature. As Hayek puts it,

> So far it has been assumed that the shape of the productivity curve [flow of outputs at each date] of the factor in question in the different stages is

10 By contrast, an increase in the demand for the product, causing its price to rise (the real wage to fall), what may be seen as a "Keynesian" case, labor input will be redeployed toward the later stages of production.

> the same. But this is not at all likely in practice. And *the actual effect of a change in the rate of interest on the price and distribution of any one factor will evidently depend on what we may call the relative interest elasticity of its productivity in the different stages*... the method adopted to give a general picture of the considerations involved is really not adequate for an exhaustive analysis. ... if we were to start from a complete restatement of the substitution relationships between all the different resources concerned, all kinds of peculiarities and apparent anomalies would appear to be quite consistent with the general tendencies which can be deduced from a cruder type of analysis. It is, for instance, quite possible that while a fall in the rate of interest will create a tendency for the services of most of the permanent factors to be invested for longer periods and for their prices to rise, in the case of some individual factor the effect may well be that it will be invested for shorter periods, or that its price will be lowered, or both.
>
> (Hayek [1941, p. 272, italics added], also quoted in Birner [1999])[11]

In retrospect, perhaps the most significant part of all this was that Hayek was implicitly embracing a measure of "time in investment" that depended on the value of investment itself, though, it seems, that the full significance of this was not seen at the time. Specifically, it was not apparent to Hayek that a value construct was available to measure the average time one has to wait to earn a dollar on any investment – a construct that was a viable simple alternative to Böhm-Bawerk's APP, and that with this construct he could have addressed many of his concerns. Interestingly, Hicks's contribution was not picked up by scholars working on this issue. It was picked up neither by advocates of the APP as an answer to their critics nor by the critics of APP as an example of how such measures should actually be constructed. We are referring to the concept of duration discussed in Part I of this work.

Capital consumption and maintenance when capital goods are heterogeneous and the future is uncertain

The recognition that any measure of time in investment depends on the rate of interest is an important instance of the more general dependence of any measure of capital on *the relative values of the production goods in question*.

11 Hayek here sees the possibility that changes in the interest rate may produce effects on the value of any investment, in terms of inputs and outputs, that are not monotonically related to those changes in the interest rate. Over some ranges that value may increase, and then decrease, and switch again, depending on the time distribution of the flow of services involved. This anticipates the main issue at the center of the third famous Cambridge–Cambridge debate, the capital controversy of the 1960s and beyond.

Hayek emphasizes that any relevant unforeseen changes will provoke changes in the *relative prices* of production goods and that this will in general lead to a reshuffling of the capital goods combinations being used in production processes. In other words, Hayek is recognizing the importance of *heterogeneity* in a way that anticipates the more systematic account of Ludwig Lachmann (discussed in the next chapter). However, it could be said that in his formal analysis, Hayek confines his attention to the "temporal" heterogeneity of the inputs. The same input at different points of time is regarded as a different entity. Changes in the relative prices of these two entities provoke changes in their quantities (the amount of any input deployed at a point in time). In this point of his analysis, inputs are treated largely as homogeneous (labor services) at different points in time, applied to fixed (though heterogeneous) capital goods. A change in the relative prices of these inputs is, in effect, a change in intertemporal values, or equivalently, a change in the relevant interest (discount, accumulation) rate. In terms of Böhm-Bawerk's simple framework, the physical inputs as well as the input values inclusive of compound interest are not invariant to the level of the interest rate.

In his general discussion, Hayek clearly realizes the complex functional heterogeneity of production goods *at any point in time*, the clear and compelling implication of which is that there is no such thing as a "quantity of capital" independent of value, that is to say, in purely quantitative terms. This is the case in spite of the fact that Hayek frequently refers, as do many others, to the "quantity" of capital, a practice that can be understood as coherent only if implicitly (and sometimes explicitly) referring to "a quantity in value terms." Without clarification, this common terminology can lead to confusion and incoherence in encouraging the reader to think of capital in terms of some measurable physical quantity.[12]

That Hayek understood this is clear from his discussion of such topics as capital consumption, accumulation, and maintenance. Hayek was, as Mises was, concerned during the 1920s and early 1930s about what they saw as the problem of capital consumption in Austria (see Hayek 1984, Chapter 6, and the references therein). Hayek (1935, 1941, Chapters 22–23) returned to this in the context of an exchange with Pigou (1935, 1941; 1932).

To answer the question of what it means to maintain the level of capital intact, one has to remember the following two principles:

1. As explained, there is no purely physical measure of capital. It is not even clear why one would want to keep capital intact in physical terms.

12 A significant example being the neoclassical production function to be discussed in the next chapter.

Any useful measure of capital is a value measure. So, maintaining capital means maintaining its *value*.

2. This being the case, we know that the capital-value of any combination, or collection, of production goods is wholly determined by the present value of its prospective flow of valuable services. So, keeping capital intact means maintaining constant its income stream in present-value terms. Capital is the stock from which income flows, the value of the stock is the (discounted) value of all of its flows.

Hayek's debate with Pigou involved disagreement over principle 1. Pigou's objective was to understand *social income* (what we call today GDP – Gross Domestic Product) and how it could be measured in a defensible way for practical applications in economic policy. But, to find such a measure requires accounting for those *aggregate* expenditures necessary to keep the productive capital resources of the nation intact. In pursuit of his investigations into *social income*, Pigou thus took an explicit aggregative approach. He wanted to provide a measure (at least in principle) of the economy's aggregate stock of capital and he looked to the *physical* items that comprised it for this purpose.[13]

For Hayek in particular, and the Austrians in general, the aggregative approach makes little sense. In all economic reasoning, one has to start from the individual and his evaluations. There was no sense in which "social" income could be understood as an entity disconnected from the incomes of the individuals who comprised the society. It is not the nation that makes an income, its individuals do. Hayek's concern was not how aggregate statistics behave during a business cycle, but how such phenomena can be connected to an individual's decisions. From Hayek's point of view, observing aggregate behavior offers a *description* of a business cycle, but not an *explanation*. Buchanan (2015) argues that, in his time, Hayek was the only economist advocating for what today is known as microfoundations.

Perhaps a clear illustration of this is the difference between physical *deterioration* and *obsolescence*. Though Pigou, for the most part, concentrates on the former, i.e., the *physical* life of the production good, when considering appropriate depreciation methods (maintenance planning), for Hayek, as for us, it is solely the latter, i.e., the useful *economic* life of the production good, that is relevant. In most cases, for durable goods, the economic life is likely to be shorter than the physical life. A tool may have only scrap value once its usefulness in production has been superseded by a later, better version, or when a

13 For a brief description of this exchange, see Lewin and Cachanosky (2019, sec. 5.2).

change in tastes, technology, or both (for example, the introduction of a new consumer good) has reduced the demand for its services. If, by contrast, the physical life of the tool is shorter than the economic life, then the physical life is in effect the economic life – the good will have to be replaced at the end of its productive–physical life).

This matter was also relevant to the Keynes–Hayek debate in the 1930s. As Horwitz (2011, p. 16) notes: "in the only real mention of the Austrian view of capital in *The General Theory*, Keynes [writes]":

> It seems probably that capital formation and capital consumption, as used by the Austrian school of economists, are not identical either with investment and disinvestment as defined above or with net investment and disinvestment. In particular, capital consumption is said to occur in circumstances where there is quite clearly no net decrease in capital equipment as defined above. I have, however, been unable to discover a reference to any passage where the meaning of these terms is clearly explained. The statement, for example, that capital formation occurs when there is a lengthening of the period of production does not much advance matters.

Horwitz (2011, p. 16) continues:

> Keynes's dismissiveness aside, this passage reveals much about the differences in approaches. Keynes seems puzzled by the Austrian claim that capital can be "consumed" even though there is no net decrease in physical capital. The answer to the puzzle is that *capital, for the Austrians, is about value, not about the physical object itself*. If we build a machine in anticipation of some specific future demand and then discover our expectations were wrong, the machine will drop in value (which is a form of capital consumption), but it does not crumple into dust. Capital goods are valued in terms of the (discounted) value of the future consumption goods they will produce. If consumer demand changes, the value of the capital good changes (assuming it is insufficiently versatile to produce whatever new product is now in demand) and capital-value is lost, thus capital has been consumed even though the physical stock of capital has not changed. This [is important in any] discussion of the business cycle. [italics added].

The appropriate procedure for the individual producer (or owner of durable goods combinations generally) who wants to maintain a given level of production (revenue income) is to anticipate as best as she can the economic life of the production components of the project and to provide for their physical maintenance, replacement, training, etc., so as to achieve this. According to Hayek, this is what should be meant by "keeping capital intact." Yet, if capital is to be understood in value terms, and such value is the present value of the capital goods cash flow, then in order to maintain capital, that income has to be constant. The issue of keeping capital constant gets pushed back to the issue of a constant flow of income.

Permanent income – it depends on what is foreseen and unforeseen

The concept of permanent income is well known in the corpus of neoclassical economics and can be traced to Hicks's classic, *Value and Capital* (Hicks, 1939, Chapter XIV). Subsequently, in an article published in 1942, the substance of which was explicitly reproduced in his *Capital and Time* (1973a, note to Chapter XIII), Hicks proposes a resolution to the dispute between Hayek and Pigou on the question of maintaining capital. In short, Hicks argues that while Hayek was essentially correct in his criticism of Pigou's approach, Hayek himself has not offered an alternative approach for the purposes of social accounting.[14]

Hayek uses Hicks's now-standard definition of income in this context, namely, "the idea of income as *the maximum rate of consumption which the recipient can enjoy and expect to continue to enjoy indefinitely*" (Scott, 1984, p. 62, italics added), sometimes referred to as "Hicksian income," but referred to by Hayek as the now-more-standard "permanent income." Yet, Hicks (1939, p. 171) expressed misgivings about this concept insofar as it renders the concepts of saving, depreciation, and investment, not

> suitable tools for any analysis which aims at logical precision. There is far too much equivocation in their meaning, equivocation which cannot be removed by the most painstaking effort. At bottom, they are not logical categories at all; they are rough approximations, used by the businessman to steer himself through the bewildering changes of situation which confront him. For this purpose, strict logical categories are not what is needed; something rougher is actually better.
>
> (also quoted in Scott [1984])

14 "Professor Hayek, on the other hand, having demolished the rival construction, fails (in my view) to provide anything solid to put in its place" (Hicks, 1942). Even in the most "subjectivist" (Austrian, Mengerian) period of his career (save for his early "Hayekian" phase) from the mid 1970s onward, Hicks remained wedded to the need to use stationary-state reasoning to discover constructs of use for aggregate analysis (and by implication economic policy?). See Lewin (1997).

In other words, the concept was too subjective for his liking[15] – but certainly not for Hayek's.

Hayek's approach can be explained as follows. Using this concept of permanent income, he analyzes cases of increasing complexity and uncertainty. In a stationary world in which the future can be accurately foreseen, including any developments that would render any productive resources economically obsolete, the problem of maintaining capital intact is a purely technical one that requires a high degree of objectivity. The simplest case is probably the one we find in *Prices and Production*, bearing in mind that along with everything else, interest-rate changes are correctly foreseen and all technical production conditions are known with certainty. In such a world, the amount of input in each period necessary to ensure the largest constant output value can be easily calculated and applied as necessary to ensure a constant flow of permanent income. The division between maintenance and production is somewhat arbitrary, but any accounting convention consistently applied to this end will suffice to define the amount necessary for capital maintenance. This is the essence of many neoclassical growth models that assume a constant depreciation rate that has to be subtracted from the compound interest rate to derive a sustainable growth path.

One can fairly easily see the consequences of relaxing these highly restrictive assumptions and allowing uncertainty regarding obsolescence, demand shifts (market conditions) and even technical conditions. The problem then becomes a highly subjective one. Expectations relating to these matters will differ across individuals. Producers and entrepreneurs have to pit their bets, their expectations, against those of others. The idea of an objectively identifiable depreciation rate or income level is untenable. Hayek notes that producers will try to take into account in their calculations all those relevant events that are foreseeable (in any degree), when taking actions to divide earnings between consumption and maintenance. However, for those that are unforeseeable this cannot be done – and Hayek might well have added that to model the situation as if this were not the case (for the purposes of social accounting or any other purpose) is a pretense of knowledge.[16]

15 Hicks (1939, p. 180): "calculations of social income [...] play [...] an important part in social statistics, and in welfare economics."

16 "[i]n a world of imperfect foresight not only the size of the capital stock, but also the income derived from it will inevitably be subject to unintended and unpredictable changes which depend on the extent and distribution of foresight, and there will be no possibility of distinguishing any particular movement of these magnitudes as normal." (Hayek, 1935, pp. 268–269). Furthermore, the occurrence of the unexpected, the unforeseen, features prominently in any Hayekian explanation of economic fluctuations. The over- and then under-maintenance of capital is the essence of a boom–bust cycle, one that leaves the economy with less capital in its wake.

In addition to these difficulties, it should be noted that, unlike Hayek's triangle situation, the flow of inputs might vary over time and that for any estimate of permanent income there may be multiple quantity-time inputs to achieve it. In other words, there may be different amounts of expenditure in each sub-period of production devoted to maintenance that would achieve the same permanent income level, so that even understood as the result of subjective calculation, the expenditure level (and time pattern) required for maintenance will generally not be unique.

Finally, the use of permanent income as a standard for comprehending capital maintenance is purely a convention, though an intuitive one. In a growing economy, it may make more sense to think in terms of a permanent growth of income, or constant *per capita* income as the relevant standard. In addition, in the individual context, the producer's objective may be one that entails a non-constant income (output) or even a non-constant growth rate. This requires a more flexible and complex calculation of what the producer's level of consumption in each period should be and what his or her investments in inputs should be in order to achieve this.

Hicks observed that in his relentless criticism of the idea of capital maintenance as a purely technical matter subject to certain articulable procedures, Hayek left "nothing solid" on which the economist might build. In our particular approach to capital pursued in this work, it is relevant to note in response to Hicks's observation that it is *precisely* because of the subjective nature of capital, permanent income, and related concepts, that *the conventions of accounting practice and financial calculation* are so important and useful. The dynamic economy in which we live is crucially dependent on the smooth function of the institution of money and no less on the institutions of accounting and finance *using monetary values*. These institutions facilitate decision-making. The ability to use financial arithmetic within an accounting framework provides producers (entrepreneurs) with the wherewithal to calculate according to their best estimates the profitability of the productive venture at hand. In acting upon this estimate, it may over time be revealed to have been right or wrong, to some degree, and this will prompt changes going forward, but, in their absence they *would not have been able to make a decision at all and would not have acted.*[17] In the absence of these institutions, which

17 This is consistent both with Hayek's later preoccupation with the function and development of all manner of "social institutions" and with his epistemological concerns relating to the subjective content of individual plans (Hayek, 1937). Institutions like money, finance and accounting provide the individual planner with shared categories that enable her to act in an uncertain world. A simple example is the preparation of a business plan to use as the basis for obtaining a business loan, and for reporting on the use of funds so obtained. High-level functioning financial markets depend on these institutions.

exist only in a for-profit private-property economy, no market process would exist, no trial-and-error speculation, or investment that is the key to social learning. Hayek's (1935) article in particular (together with similar work from this period) is an important complement to both Lachmann's discussion of point-of-time capital heterogeneity, as well as Mises's financial approach to capital to be discussed in Chapter 6.

Chapter 5

Ludwig Lachmann and the capital structure

The heterogeneity of production goods and the Austrian School

Ludwig Lachmann, a student of Hayek's at the London School of Economics (LSE) in the 1930s, had begun working on the problems that Hayek wrestled with in capital theory in the 1940s. This work was ultimately crystalized in his *Capital and its Structure* (1956). His capital theory provides the definitive understanding of the nature and working of the capital structure for current work by Austrians, through its reference to the nature of capital heterogeneity. Rather than conceiving of production as involving a homogeneous mass of "capital" as a stock (as in both the neoclassical and modern Ricardian conceptions), Lachmann sees it as involving an ordered structure of heterogeneous multi-specific complementary production goods. This structure is ever-changing as entrepreneurs combine and recombine productive resources in accordance with their assessments of profitability. Profit and loss continually reshape the production structure in accordance with the revealed preferences of consumers. In different ways, both Lachmann and Mises (the subject of the next chapter) move back closer to the original version of Carl Menger (subjectivity in capital theory).

Although Böhm-Bawerk's APP has no defensible application to real-world production processes, the essential idea is still relevant and is actually a precursor of much work done on the nature of production in the modern world, including the neoclassical production function. Böhm-Bawerk tried to capture, in quantitative terms, the average amount of time taken in any production project – and from this it was but a small step to seeing it as a purely physical measure of capital. His approach invites the interpretation that time is a metric for reducing heterogeneous capital goods (production goods) to a common denominator. In a sense capital is time, production is time.

By contrast, Lachmann maintained that, outside of equilibrium, there was simply no way to aggregate the bewildering array of heterogeneous production goods. In reality, capital is not a *stock* of anything. It is, rather, a *structure* of different things fitting together to serve the purposes of their employers. In one of his most famous quotes, Lachmann explains:

> The generic concept of capital without which economists cannot do their work has no measurable counterpart among material objects; it reflects the entrepreneurial appraisal of such objects. Beer barrels and blast furnaces, harbor installations and hotel room furniture are capital not by virtue of their physical properties but by virtue of their economic functions. Something is capital because the market, the consensus of entrepreneurial minds, regards it as capable of yielding an income… [though heterogeneous in nature] the stock of capital used by society does not present a picture of chaos. Its arrangement is not arbitrary. There is some order to it.
>
> (Lachmann, 1956, p. xv)

The fact that capital stock is heterogeneous does not mean it has to be disordered. The various components of the capital structure stand in sensible relationship to one another because they perform *specific* functions *together*. They are used in various capital combinations. Horwitz (2011, p. 5) describes capital heterogeneity as pieces of a jigsaw puzzle that can be combined in limited but different ways to produce a number of shapes. If we understand the logic of capital combinations, we give meaning to the capital structure and, in this way, we are able to design appropriate economic policies or, even more importantly, avoid inappropriate ones (for example Lachmann [1947, 1956, p. 123]).

Understanding capital combinations entails an understanding of the concepts of *complementarity* and *substitutability*. These concepts pertain to a world in which observed prices are actual (disequilibrium) prices, in the sense that they reflect inconsistent expectation and in which changes that occur cause protracted visible adjustments. Capital goods are complements if they contribute together to a given *production plan*. A production plan is defined by the pursuit of a given set of ends to which the production goods are the means. As long as the plan is being successfully fulfilled, all the production goods stand in complementary relationship to one another. They are part of the same plan. The complementarity relationships within the plan may be quite intricate and no doubt will involve different stages of production and distribution.

Substitution occurs when a production plan fails (in whole or in part). When some element of the plan fails, a contingency adjustment must be sought. Some resources must be substituted for others. This is the role, for example, of spare parts, or excess inventory. Thus, complementarity, and substitutability are properties of different states of the world. The same good can be a complement in one situation and a substitute in another.[1]

Ultimately, even though the complementarity, and substitutability of goods may be constrained by their physical characteristics, it is a subjective assessment of the entrepreneur's vision as to how different resources may or may not be combined. Substitutability can only be gauged to the extent that a certain set of contingency events can be visualized. There may be some events, such as those caused by significant technological changes, that not having been predictable, render some production plans valueless. The resources associated with them will have to be incorporated into some other production plan or else scrapped – they will have been rendered unemployable. This is a natural result of economic progress that is driven primarily by the trial-and-error discovery of new and superior outputs and techniques of production. What determines the fate of any capital good in the face of change is the extent to which it can be fitted into any other capital combination without loss in value. The extent to which it can maintain its value in alternative combinations is a measure of its degree of substitutability. Capital goods are regrouped, and those that lose their value completely are scrapped. That is, capital goods, though heterogeneous and diverse, are often capable of performing a number of different economic functions. They are multi-specific (which means they are neither perfectly substitutable with no loss of value, nor perfectly specific with total loss of value in the face of change).

Within the plan of a single organization, production goods may appear in a *planned complementary* relationship to one another. The role of the entrepreneur consists in forming and reforming profitable capital combinations. At a higher level, the different plans of different production organizations (firms) exhibit an *unplanned complementarity* that is the result of the market process (Adam Smith's invisible hand or Hayek's spontaneous order). This spontaneous order is brought about by the functioning of the price system providing profit-and-loss signals and incentives.

The *degree of specificity* can be thought of as another "dimension" in relation to capital goods. Capital goods are economic goods by virtue of the *purpose* they are made to serve by the entrepreneur. Money is the least specific, most general, while some have multiple possible purposes all the way to those

1 Lachmann (1947, p. 199, 1956, p. 56) uses the example of a delivery company. The company possesses a number of delivery vans. Each one is a complement to the others in that they cooperate to fulfill an overall production plan. That plan encompasses the routine completion of a number of different delivery routes. As long as the plan is being fulfilled, this relationship prevails, but if one of the vans should break down, one or more of the others may be diverted in order to compensate for the unexpected loss of the use of one of the productive resources. To that extent and in that situation, they are substitutes.

that have only a single purpose. Money may be thought of as a kind of "general purpose technology." Money is *specified* into concrete capital goods.[2]

The macroeconomic implications of heterogeneity, investment, and technological change

Lachmann's work on capital was done in the context of the Keynesian revolution. He was at the time at the LSE, the center of the Hayekian opposition to the Cambridge Keynesians. In a 1948 article he specifically discusses the implications of his view of capital for Keynes's approach.

> The modern theory of investment, set forth by Lord Keynes in *The General Theory,* has had its many triumphs these last 12 years, but it still has a number of gaps. Conceiving of investment as simple growth of a stock of homogeneous capital, it is ill-equipped to cope with situations in which the immobility of heterogeneous capital resources imposes a strain on the economic system. In particular, it can tell us little about the "inducement to invest" in a world where scarcity of some capital resources co-exists with abundance of others.
>
> (Lachmann, 1948, p. 698)

Lachmann (1948) then proceeds to lay out a detailed analysis of the implications of capital heterogeneity, perhaps even more fully and clearly than in his earlier 1947 article on complementarity and substitutability (Lachmann, 1947). He links these concepts to the theory of investment (which he points out must contain an implicit theory of capital) and specifically to Keynes's marginal-efficiency concept (which lacks any recognition of such a theory). Anticipating his future preoccupations, he also explores the role of changing and inconsistent expectations and points out that this implies the enduring existence of disequilibrium.

Perhaps the most important general implication of a disequilibrium approach to capital is the proposition that *capital accumulation very often entails technological change*. Most technical change is embodied in new (improved) capital goods, involves the production of new consumption goods, or both. It is very likely that government expenditure "crowds out" not only private-sector investment, but also *private-sector investment-induced technical progress*. The shape of the capital structure will be different and, because capital assets are heterogeneous, specific, and durable, it will remain different from what it would otherwise have been.

2 A discussion with Bill Tulloh is gratefully acknowledged. In the context of ABCT those capital combinations with production-goods with a high degree of specificity will be more likely to be subject to capital losses than those with more adaptable production goods.

Given that capital accumulation and technological progress go together, Lachmann recasts Böhm-Bawerk's intuition about increasing roundaboutness into the idea of increasing *complexity*. Production goods are heterogeneous and exist in a structure of production that becomes more complex and heterogeneous with economic progress. Lachmann's theory is a theory of progress reflected in and achieved by a continuing specialization of economic activities. Heterogeneity matters because heterogeneous capital goods perform *qualitatively* different functions and they do so in combination with other human and physical resources.

New goods, new methods of production, new modes of organization, new resources (production goods) (Schumpeter, 1942, pp. 84–85) – all of these are part of the market process, all this change is part of the "information age." It is not simply the fact of changes in technology that is revolutionary; it is the speed with which it is occurring that is new. The pace of change is not only quicker, it is accelerating. Lachmann's considerations suggest, however, that our ability to absorb and adjust to change has dramatically increased; it must have, or else we would not be able to observe these changes, occurring as they do within a well-ordered social framework, a framework that remains intact in spite of the ubiquity and accelerating speed of change.

To understand the phenomenon of accelerating structural change occurring together with our enhanced abilities to adapt to change, we must realize that *the scope and pace of technological change is governed by our ability to generate and process relevant information*. This means that the current pace of technical change is dependent on the results of past technical advances, particularly the ability to generate and process information. This is a complex process involving multilevel interactions over time. If technological change is seen as the result of many trial-and-error selections (of production processes, of product types, of modes of distribution, and so on) then the ability to generate and perceive more possibilities will result in a greater number of successes. It will, of course, also result in a greater number of failures. Lachmann's proposition that capital accumulation, proceeding as it does hand in hand with technological change, implies that it brings with it capital regrouping as a result of failed production plans. Failure is necessary in order for social learning to occur.

Lachmann's contributions to Austrian capital theory in relation to "capital as finance"

While it is true that Lachmann's (like Hayek's) discussions in capital theory are preoccupied with physical, objective, production processes, and the resources they involve, the implicit message throughout is about the *value* of these resources as organized and deployed by the producer–entrepreneur.

Profit is the objective. And to earn profit, value must be imputed to the resources in the form of an income stream from the output they produce. This is what makes anything part of "capital" rather than simply its physical characteristics. The value attributed to any production good is the projection of the subjective appraisal by the entrepreneur of its potential to produce (together with complementary resources) something of value greater than what it costs to acquire and use. There is a clear connection between a consideration of the physical form of the capital structure and the notion of profitability.

Having said this, it remains true that Lachmann (like Hayek, but unlike Mises – see the next chapter), is not explicit about the notion of "capital" as distinct from "capital goods" and, although there is some discussion of financial assets in *Capital and its Structure* (1956, Chapter 6), he does not spell out clearly the role of financial calculation (for example present-value estimation) by the decision-maker. In this, he is no different from most of the Austrians. Where they do mention it, it is always in passing. The clearest statement by Lachmann is perhaps the following:

> ... capital goods have a *value dimension* as well as their physical dimension. While in terms of the latter capital is of course heterogeneous, in terms of the former diverse capital goods may be *reduced to homogeneity.* In fact, in planning and carrying out plans *this has to be done since the planner has to match means with ends* and, except for sums of money, almost all his means are capital goods. He has to *evaluate* them in order to make them commensurable to each other as well as to his ends. Every plan, simply for the sake of the comparability of the means it employs, has to *assign values* to its capital inputs. Plan failure and consequent revision will probably entail changes in the evaluation of capital goods, but it is a peculiar aspect of our problem that even while the plan proceeds satisfactorily with no unexpected change in the workshop or market, planners may have reason to change capital-values. Changes in the value dimension may not be accompanied by any other observable event.
>
> (Lachmann, 1986, p. 79, italics added)

And earlier he says: "We might say of course that the firm will act in such a manner as to maximize the present value of its expected future income stream," but he immediately adds, "but such a description ... is of little use to us." (Lachmann, 1986, p. 64).

In addition, in his consideration of the phenomenon of *capital maintenance*, Lachmann adopts the approach (citing Hayek, 1935) that maintenance entails keeping the capitalized-*value* of the expected income stream intact (as discussed in the previous chapter). This implies using a value approach to the estimation of depreciation and resort to accounting and financial conventions. In somewhat confusing terminology, Lachmann explains as follows: "Capital could be said to maintain its quantity while altering its form only if the maintenance of its value, while it is embodied in each of these forms, could be assured" (Lachmann, 1986, p. 71) and further, "Maintaining the value of capital resources is an important economic function." (Lachmann, 1986, p. 73).

Conceiving capital this way, which means as the result of a subjective evaluation process of productive resources, compels a consideration of the nature of productive labor, or, what we today call human capital. Lachmann, again in common with the other Austrians, never uses this term, nor considers human capital in the same analytical category as physical capital. Passing statements do, however, indicate his awareness of the issue. For example:

> It goes without saying that in the real world it will hardly be possible to produce a new good, or vary effectively the character of an existing one, without varying the *blend of skills required* in the labor force, or the composition of raw material input used. Similarly, any change in the latter or the *composition of the labor force* is bound to have some effect on output. But it is no less true that there can be hardly a significant change in output or labor or raw material input which does not necessitate a regrouping of the capital combination with or without new investment.
>
> (Lachmann [1986, pp. 64–65, italics added]), see also Lachmann (1956, p. 49)

It should be clear that from the perspective of the decision-maker evaluating productive resources in general, there is no *categorical* difference between physical and human resources. There are, of course, enormous *practical* differences associated with their employment and management, given that human resources have agency and dealing with them entails forming a relationship that is absent in the case of the employment of physical resources. Yet, in terms of calculating the capital-value of the firm and its "capital combinations," the potential contribution of labor (the human capital available to it) has to be included in the same way as those of physical productive goods.

Relating to the broader framework adopted in this work, Lachmann's work adds considerable detail concerning the problem of purchasing and renting heterogeneous yet complementary goods by the entrepreneur in charge of a production process.

Problems with the aggregate production function

Lachmann's consideration on the problem of heterogeneity and aggregation have serious implications for formal analysis in economics. These are not just marginal semantic issues. The argument can be made that the aggregate production function is built on ultimately inconsistent assumptions. As we show below, this issue has been known for decades because of the work of Franklin Fisher and his collaborators.

Notwithstanding its continued widespread use in theoretical and empirical studies in the neoclassical economics framework, the criticism of the aggregate production function is fundamental. This criticism involves the claim that it relies on a flawed general aggregation logic (see Fisher and Monz (1993) and Felipe and Fisher (2006) for the most recent review). A summary must suffice here to give the flavor of the overall critique.

Following F.M. Fisher (2005), imagine that a production process can be characterized by a function of the form represented in Equation 5.1.

$$q = f(k,l) \qquad 5.1$$

Where q is the output and k and l are the factors of production. Knowing the values of the *quantities* of k and l, one can accurately predict the *quantity* of q that will be produced. Imagine further that there are φ firms such that

$$q_z = f(\boldsymbol{k}_z, \boldsymbol{l}_z); z = 1 \ldots \varphi,; \qquad 5.2$$

Where $\boldsymbol{k} = k_i, (i = 1, \ldots, n)$ and $\boldsymbol{l} = l_j, (j = 1, \ldots, m)$. In Equation 5.2, $\boldsymbol{k}_z$ and $\boldsymbol{l}_z$ are vectors of *different* types of production goods and labor used in the z firms. Now consider Equation 5.3

$$Q = F(K,L) \qquad 5.3$$

Where Q, K, and L are composite (aggregates) purportedly measuring the *quantity* of production, *quantity* of capital employed, and *quantity* of labor employed.[3] There are φ consumption goods (each produced by a different firm), n types of production goods, and m types of labor services.

3 More accurately, it is the *services* of capital and labor that are the inputs into production. K and L are stocks that when employed yield a flow of services per period of time. The last point raises the important question of why K (production goods) alone has been seen to be problematic in relation to the aggregation problem. The answer to this question goes to the very meaning of the concept of "capital" as used in economics and is central to our work here.

The above-mentioned literature considers the following questions:

1. Under what condition does Equation 5.1 make sense? This is not a trivial question. Clearly, k and l must be homogeneous identifiable entities whose services can be measured per period of time (the question that Böhm-Bawerk raised that triggered so much criticism). If, by contrast, k and l are heterogeneous collections, an aggregation problem exists *even at this project level*. Further, if more than one output is jointly produced, then there is a problem of aggregating output.
2. Under which conditions, and how, can we go from Equation 1.2 to Equation 1.3? This is the better-known question of the two. The answer given by Fisher and others is as clear as it is uncompromising: except under the most unusual circumstances, such aggregation *is not possible*. In addition, this applies even if one assumes macro-equilibrium.

Even at the micro- or firm level, and even assuming well-behaved micro-production functions with homogenous inputs, the conditions for successful across-firm aggregation are vanishingly likely to be met. First, there must be a state of *perpetual* long-run equilibrium. Second, if not in equilibrium, there must be *universal* constant returns to scale. Third,

> even under constant returns to scale, the conditions for aggregation are so stringent as to make the existence of aggregate production functions in real economies a non-event. This is true not only for the existence of an aggregate capital stock but also for the existence of such constructs as aggregate labor or even aggregate output.
>
> (Fisher 2005, 489)[4]

Given these serious limitations of the aggregate production function, how is it possible that the production function is used in empirical work? Why is there a "close fit" between the earnings of capital and labor and the estimated Cobb–Douglas production functions? According to Felipe and McCombie (2014) there is no mystery about this. Consider the aggregate accounting identity in Equation 5.4

4 Successful aggregation would mean that the aggregate production function that resulted, behaved as the neoclassical theory says it should, with the input categories, like K and L , providing unambiguous information about the variation of the components of these categories. K and L will behave like quantities of identifiable factors of production contributing marginal products (in terms of variations in the aggregate output) and for which there are the expected downward sloping demand curves. Realizing this, it is perhaps not surprising that aggregate production functions are never likely to be found in the real-world.

$$Q = wL + rK \tag{5.4}$$

Where Q is the *value* of final output, such as real GDP, L is the constant-price-index aggregate of labor, K is the constant-price-index aggregate of "capital," w is the average wage of a unit of L, and r is the rental-rate of a unit of K.

Proceed first by totally differentiating this identity, then $dlog\ (Q)$ $= \left(\frac{wL}{Q}\right) dlog(L) + \left(\frac{rK}{Q}\right) dlog(K) = \alpha \cdot dlog(L) + (1-\alpha) \cdot dlog(K)$.

Parameter α is the income-share of L and $(1 - \alpha)$ is the income-share of K. Integrating this equation gives Equation 5.5

$$Q = AL^{a} K^{1-a} \tag{5.5}$$

Where A represents the constant of integration. This looks just like a Cobb–Douglas production function with constant returns to scale. It is important to be clear, $Q = AL^{\alpha} K^{1-\alpha}$ *is not* an approximation of $Q = wL + rK$, it is an *exact transformation*. Thus, it is to be expected that the Cobb–Douglas production function would give a "good fit" for income shares. This means that the Cobb–Douglas production function does not explain factor-share, it only expresses them in a *different* way. A "good fit" does not solve the heterogeneity issue, nor suggest that it is irrelevant.

> While, over some restricted range of the data, approximations may appear to fit, good approximations to the true underlying technical relations require close approximation to the stringent aggregation conditions, ... this is not a sensible thing to suppose. ... When one works – as one must at an aggregate level – with *quantities measured in value terms*, the appearance of a well-behaved aggregate production function tells one nothing at all about whether there really is one. Such an appearance stems from the accounting identity that relates the value of outputs to the value of inputs – *nothing more*.
>
> (Fisher, 2005, p. 490, first set of italics added)

The italicized phrase "quantities measured in value terms" is noteworthy – this, indeed, is the root of all capital controversies. Consideration of the fundamentals underlying the capital concepts in current use, both from the Mengerian–Austrian perspective and from a critical neoclassical perspective, suggest a different approach is called for. Some scholars, such as Irving Fisher

(1906) and Frank Fetter (1977) realized the extent of the problems and implicitly offered a solution by adopting a different approach to capital. They are not alone. As mentioned above, Ludwig von Mises focused on the role of capital as used in "ordinary" business life and on its role in facilitating decision-making through accounting and calculation (see Braun et al. [2016]). Capital as a financial value is a tool for coping with the undeniable bewildering heterogeneity of productive resources. It is what enables us to make decisions despite the multi-specificity of most capital goods. This is the topic of the next chapter.

Chapter 6

Ludwig von Mises and capital from a financial perspective

Mises's financial view of capital

Unlike his other well-known Austrian colleagues, Ludwig von Mises never produced a work devoted solely to an exploration of the meaning of capital or its role in the economy.[1] This was the case, notwithstanding the fact that he is the originator of the ABCT in *The Theory of Money and Credit* (1912), which combines capital theory with Wicksell's natural rate of interest. Furthermore, Mises took no part in any capital controversy nor even wrote about them. Mises's views on capital must be gleaned from his works devoted to other specific topics in which aspects related to capital theory are discussed. To infer what his thoughts on capital are requires an indirect approach as well as some familiarity with the role he assigns to institutions in the market process. Yet, his views on capital are interesting and highly suggestive in a way that has been underappreciated.[2] In fact, Mises's view is consistent with the discussion in Part III and, as will then become clear, therefore also consistent with the discussion in Part I as well.

While most Austrians develop their work on capital following Böhm-Bawerk's groundwork, Mises followed Menger more closely than he did Böhm-Bawerk. Both in his treatise on socialism (1922, p. 123) and in his *magnus opus*, *Human Action* (1949, p. 262), he followed the common practice of the business world in defining capital as an amount of money required to start, expand, or run a business. For Mises, capital is a sum of money (market values) obtained following accounting practices.

1 In addition to those already discussed see Kirzner (1996).

2 Braun's (2015, 2017) work suggests that Mises's position is arguably foreshadowed in a neglected article by Menger (1888). According to Braun, Menger opposed all attempts to define capital as something physical and argued that capital should be understood as a value construct. Yet, Menger does not do much more than offer a criticism of capital in physical terms. What capital theory should look like is not specified.

> Capital is the sum of the money equivalent of all assets minus the sum of the money equivalent of all liabilities as dedicated at a definite date to the conduct of the operations of a definite business unit. It does not matter in what these assets may consist, whether they are pieces of land, buildings, equipment, tools, goods of any kind, and order, claims, receivables, cash, or whatever.
>
> (Mises, 1949, p. 262)

True to his subjectivism, for Mises it is not physical characteristics that determine whether a given asset is part of capital or not. Rather, it is how the entrepreneur *sees* the asset that determines its role as part of capital (Lewin, 1998).[3]

Mises would prefer not to use the term "capital" in any way to denote physical production goods. But given the common usage, he considers that at least we ought to distinguish carefully between "capital" and "capital goods." We "may *acquiesce* in the terminological usage of calling the produced factors of production capital goods. *But this does not render the concept of real [physical] capital any more meaningful.*" (Mises, 1949, p. 263, italics added).

> From the notion of capital goods one must clearly distinguish the concept of capital. The concept of capital is the fundamental concept of economic calculation, the foremost mental tool of the conduct of affairs in the market economy.
>
> (Mises, 1949, p. 260, italics added)[4]

Capital goods are "intermediary stations on the way leading from the very beginning of production to its final goal, the turning out of consumer's goods" (Mises, 1949, p. 490).[5] While it is true that the entrepreneur subjectively "aggregates" the combination of production goods used over time in the production process to come up with an estimated money-value of the project, for Mises, the aggregation of capital goods (usually denoted in neoclassical economics as K)

3 Note the tension already mentioned in our earlier discussion. Mises defines capital as balance-sheet "equity," yet, the factor of production quality of any asset depends on how it is seen by the entrepreneur and how it is used. It does not depend on the ownership of said asset. A tool is a "capital good" regardless of whether it is owned by the owner of the firm or it is loaned (rented) from someone else. As discussed in Part I, the value of rented assets is reflected in the value on the balance sheet attributed to owned assets and thus indirectly enters into "equity."

4 For a discussion of possible ambiguities in Mises conception of the nature of capital in various works of his see Braun et al. (2016), and Lewin and Cachanosky (2019, sec. 7.2).

5 For an extended discussion of this concept of capital goods as part of the "unfinished plans" of entrepreneurs see Kirzner (2010).

understood as an agglomeration of physical capital in some objective sense, is an "empty concept" and a "mythical" notion (Mises, 1949, p. 263).

Even though, in Mises's terms "capital goods" is a misnomer, the term "capital" is actually of significant relevance in both market theory and in the practice of running a business. To understand this dichotomy, and in particular how "capital" is a useful concept, it is important to understand Mises's historical and institutional approach.

Capital as a historically specific concept

Capital, in Mises's view, is a basic and indispensable tool of economic calculation used by entrepreneurs in capitalist economies (market economies). For Mises, "capital" is an *historically specific* concept:

> The concept of capital cannot be separated from the context of monetary calculation and from the social structure of a market economy in which alone monetary calculation is possible. It is a concept which *makes no sense outside the conditions of a market economy*. It plays a role exclusively in the plans and records of individuals acting on their own account in such a system of private ownership of the means of production, and it developed with the spread of economic calculation in monetary terms.
>
> (Mises, 1949, p. 262, italics added)

Monetary calculation based on capital is only possible under capitalism. With the tools of capital accounting, entrepreneurs are able to compare the economic significance of their inputs and their outputs even in a complicated and dynamically "changing industrial economy" (Mises, 1949, p. 511). Entrepreneurs try to *compare* the market valuation of a set of factors of production with the value they think said factors of production can have under their management. That is what distinguishes a capitalist society from its alternatives. Without access to capital valuation, an alternative method is needed to decide how to allocate resources (for instance, intuition, or the central planner's best guess). This is consistent with his criticism of socialism, where the absence of market prices would make "rational" economic calculation impossible.

> [O]nly people who are in a position to resort to monetary calculation can evolve to full clarity the distinction between an economic substance [capital] and the advantages derived from it [income], and can apply it neatly to all classes, kinds, and orders of goods, and services.
>
> (Mises, 1949, p. 261)

Mises's theory of capital is not a theory of how tools play their role in a production function. It is, rather, an institutional theory. In his view, understanding capital involves understanding the way monetary calculation, based on (financial) capital allows entrepreneurs to organize the production process under capitalism. Capital is not an input into the production function, it is a prerequisite for the economic calculation required to decide *what* and *how* to produce. Thus, Mises's approach makes it clear that even though "financial capital" and "capital goods" may share the word "capital," the conceptual difference between them is crucial for an understanding of the role of capital in a market economy. Mises's theory of capital is a theory of capitalism, a theory of how entrepreneurial operations are guided by capital accounting.

As we mentioned, Mises does not have a work specifically devoted to the theory of capital. His views on the matter are spread out within his voluminous body of work. It may be argued that Mises's take on the theory of capital as finance is rudimentary and needs further elaboration (see for example Braun, 2017). Yet, Mises is not alone in his approach to capital. Notably Fetter (1977) and I. Fisher (1906) have a similar understanding. What is perhaps unique in Mises, is the institutional use he has for the term "capital" and the role it plays in his criticism of socialism. This is understandable given the central role he played in the socialist calculation debate in the early twentieth century. Without the possibility of resorting to monetary calculation, inputs and outputs could not be reduced to a common denominator and an industrial economy would not be sustainable. Hence, the impossibility under socialism to economize on resources and to determine where input factors can be employed more economically (more on this in Chapter 9).

> [I]t lies in the very nature of socialist production that the shares of the particular factors of production in the national dividend cannot be ascertained, and that it is impossible in fact to gauge the relationship between expenditure [production effort] and income [production proceeds].
>
> (Mises, 1920, p. 2) [brackets contain translations in Braun et al. (2016)]

A socialist government, understood as that government directing production in the absence of private property of the means of production, would need what the capitalist system has, namely, the concepts of capital, and income to guide its operations. However, without private property on factors of production, the concepts of capital and income are "mere postulates devoid of any practical application" (Mises, 1949, p. 264); see also Murphy (2015, pp. 223–246).

Capital and production

If capital is not a physical phenomenon, but, rather a conceptual one measured in terms of (actual or estimated) market value, then it is obviously subjective in nature. Different investors or entrepreneurs, with different production processes in mind, may consider the same assets in different ways. For some of them certain assets may be part of the project's capital, while for others it may not. Not only do different combinations of physical assets that are *seen* as capital vary, but the valuation of the same assets as seen by different investors will vary. The investor and entrepreneur compare the value they *think* capital can have (under their control) versus the value attached to them by the market (where such valuations exist). Only in the particular case of equilibrium, where all profit opportunities are exploited and all expectations are identical (and correct), does capital-value have any kind of "objective" measure. Capital, and its value, cannot be detached from the income (measured in present-value terms) it is *expected* to produce. Capital is the value attached to *all* factors of production (tools, labor, land, etc.) used to produce a cash flow. The implications for capital as an aggregate construct of productive assets should be clear.

A way to think about these issues is to consider that capital has three different, yet inseparable, dimensions: value, quantity, and time.[6] The combination of heterogeneous factors of production have value to the extent of the market value of their output. It should also be clear that to think in terms of capital in financial terms *does not* mean that physical capital (tools, etc.) do not exist or are irrelevant. The question is whether the former is the proper and exclusive way to think about capital or it is not. We can lay out the deployment of capital as shown in Figure 6.1.

There is an initial amount of financial capital, K_0, that is used to purchase and rent factors of production. Then these resources are combined in specific ways to produce other intermediate goods or consumption goods. This process starts in period $t = 0$ and ends in period $t = n$. For the entrepreneur standing in $t = 0$, the value of all the factors of production to be used (the capital) equals the present value of the services (expected outputs) of these assets ($K_0 = PV(k_0)$), which includes the market value added (MVA) – i.e., what the entrepreneur thinks can be added to their original estimated market value. To the extent that this entrepreneur is correct in his or her assessment, the entrepreneur then adds value to the stock of factors of production by discovering and implementing alternative and more profitable uses of them.

6 To be more precise, there are just two dimensions, quantity and value, that occur together in time (quantity-time and value-time). Historically, in economics, most of the work has focused on the former, this work focuses more on the latter.

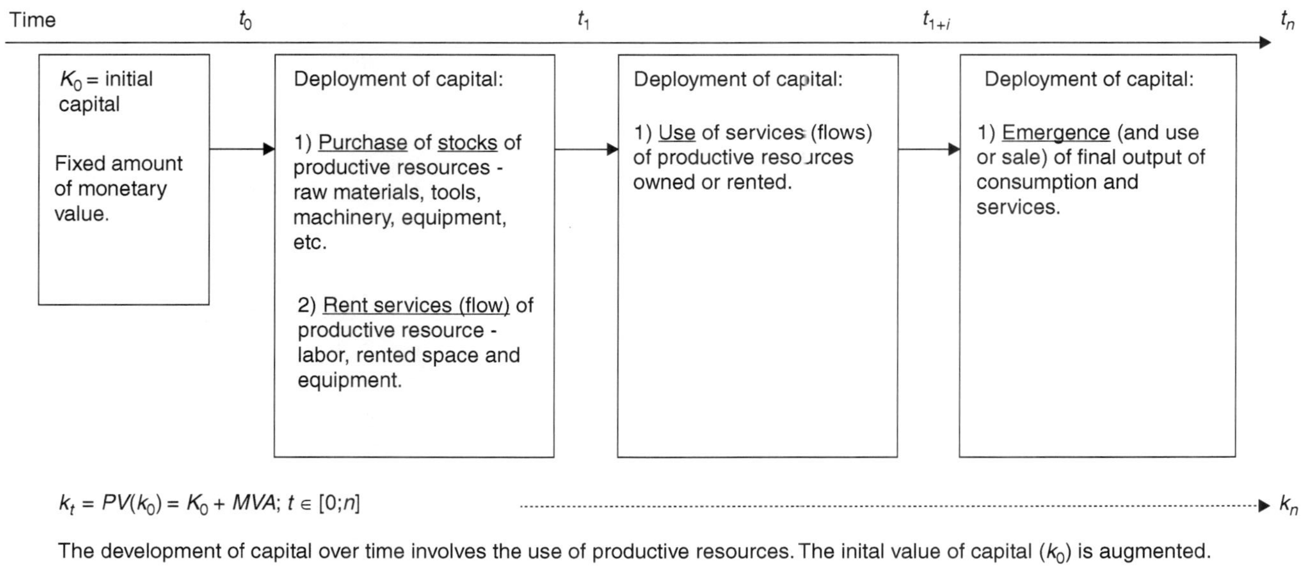

Figure 6.1 The deployment of capital over time.
Source: Lewin and Cachanosky (2019, Fig. 1).

We will return to the relationship between the entrepreneur and MVA in Chapter 9.

Conclusion

Mises's views on capital are important for understanding how capital functions in real-world economies. We may say that Mises puts capital back into capitalism and explains why its absence in centrally planned economies deprives those economies of prosperity. It puts entrepreneurial calculation front and enter for an understanding of the economic process. There are no market entrepreneurs without capital markets, and without market entrepreneurs the economy stagnates or collapses. A reorientation among economists interested in capital toward an adoption of Mises's perspective, while integrating it into the already existing and important understanding of the connection between production structure and time, would be, in our opinion, a great advance.

In addition, Mises's approach provides the opportunity to connect the economist's understanding of capital with the finance scholar's understanding of capital. They are two dimensions of the same phenomenon. Mises does not provide this connection. The view of capital as money finance is not clearly connected by him to the calibration of time in the calculation process. Mises refers to the need of the entrepreneur to engage in subjective monetary calculation, but he does not explain how this is done. For example, he does not indicate *how* the time-value of money weighs in that calculation, except to say that it does. And the connection between this and the "amount" of time involved in any production process or investment is not perceived. It seems only one economist saw this clearly, John Hicks, and his early contribution was ignored, not only by the Austrians, but also by all other economists. This is the subject of the next chapter.

Chapter 7

John Hicks and capital in the aggregate production function

John Hicks's neo-Austrian capital framework: time is irreversible

The use of the word "capital" means different things in economics and finance. This is the result of a turn in economics toward using the word to mean physical production goods, whereas in finance the word refers to the money-value of investment of all kinds (as discussed in the previous chapter). The capital concept used in economics thus deviated considerably over the years from that used in finance and in the world of business. Notably, most of this change occurred in the literature on growth theory and microeconomic production theory. Bridging these different uses, as we attempt to do in this book, can provide benefits for both strands of literature: economics, and finance.[1]

A well-known economist, maybe the only economist, who also considered this issue was John Hicks. In fact, in his later work, Hicks returned to an "Austrian" approach to capital and provided a framework that is essentially financial in character. Most of Hicks's contributions in this area, however, remained unnoticed.

Hicks (1939, 1965, 1973a) has written extensively on capital. Besides these three well-known books, his contribution also includes a number of articles on capital theory. He repeatedly returned to problems of capital theory during his career, but not always with the same answers.[2] However, an enduring characteristic of Hicks's writing is that most of his informal discussion contains

1 The original inspiration for the development of this framework dates to Lewin (1997a) and Lewin (1999, Chapter 6). Some years later, after developing a familiarity with the notion of bond duration, D , (and Hicks's AP) we saw how Hicks's framework could be more fully utilized to integrate economic and financial perspectives.

2 "Capital (I am not the first to discover) is a very large subject, with many aspects; wherever one starts, it is hard to bring more than a few of them into view. It is just as if one were making pictures of a building; though it is the same building, it looks quite different from different angles. As I now realize, I have been walking round my subject, taking different views of it" (Hicks, 1973a, p. v).

valuable insights. These informal discussions include remarks on the role of time in production, particularly in his *Capital and Time* (1973a) (see also Hicks, 1973b, 1976, 1979). His concern with the role of time in production accompanied a revived interest in Austrian capital theory (see Lewin, 1997), from where we draw the material in this section). Hicks referred to his new approach to capital as *neo-Austrian*, which shows his long-standing engagement with the Austrian literature. As we discuss below, Hicks's work fits nicely with financial concepts that are the basis of the analysis in this book.

Hicks starts by pointing out the importance of the "irreversibility of time" and the certainty of the past and the uncertainty of the future. The past is known in a way that the future is not. This is a crucial difference that plays a central role in any investment decision. What is known today used to be the unknown future at some point in the past. For Hicks (1976, p. 264), this has implications for time-series analysis that are sometimes overlooked. The fact that data is arranged in a time-series format does not mean the data is actually *in* real time. For instance, today the past relationship between years nine and ten looks like the relationship between years eight and nine. However, in year nine the information of year eight was known data, but the information of year ten was still unknown. Hicks (1976, p. 265) sees an implication of this in the valuation of assets or stocks. The issue is that as time goes by, the *value* of assets or stocks may change as uncertain information (expectations) become past data.[3]

Subjectivizing Hicks's simple conceptual framework

Even though (as discussed in Chapter 1), Hicks offers a solution to Böhm-Bawerk's APP that is today known as Macaulay duration, he shared general skepticism about the soundness of the Böhm-Bawerkian "period of production." Hicks (1973a, pp. 98–99) notes that all production is the joint result of cooperating productive resources. The contribution of a single capital good to a stream of output cannot be assigned to a specific final unit of output.

3 We arrange past data in time-series, but our time series are not fully in time. The relation of year 9 to year 10 looks like its relation to year 8; but in year 9 year 10 was future while year 8 was past. The actions of year 9 were based, or could be based, upon knowledge of year 8; but not on knowledge of year 10, only on guesses about year 10. For in year 9 the knowledge that we have about year 10 did not yet exist.

(Hicks, 1976, p. 264, italics added)

The value that is set upon the opening stock depends in part upon the value which is expected, at the beginning of the year, for the closing stock; but there may be things which were included in the opening stock because, in the light of information then available, they seemed to be valuable; but at the end of the year it is clear that they are not valuable, so they have to be excluded. This may well mean that the net investment of year 1, calculated at the end of year 1, was over-valued – at least it seems to be over-valued from the standpoint of year 2.

(Hicks, 1976, p. 265)

Therefore, the average period of production cannot be properly estimated. In other words, the value of the final good at any moment in time is not the simple summation of the value added by the inputs up to that moment, since those inputs are also contributing at the same time to a number of different final goods that will be available at different times. For Hicks, and as noted by other authors, the imputation of units of output to particular factor inputs is not possible when there is fixed capital involved without resorting to some arbitrary solution (such as an accounting rule or convention).

Hicks (1973a, p. 100) reiterates the criticism of the average period of production as a *physical* measure. Yet, he strongly affirms the importance of Menger's and Böhm-Bawerk's insights, which should not be abandoned. After all, production does take time. And since time is involved in the production process, there is such a thing as a "production (capital) structure" that captures how the different factors of production are combined together and ordered in different periods of time to yield an orderly production process. A production process can be understood as a stream of inputs that produces a stream of outputs. *How* these inputs are combined and sequentially applied is the *technique* (technology) applied in the *production process*. If this stream of inputs and output is expressed in value terms, then what we have is a typical cash flow of a business project.

Hicks offers a financial framework to analyze the value of capital. In this case, what is necessary for a potential project to be profitable, or viable, depends on its present value. For any project, the discounted cash flow is the net present value (NPV). This value should be positive at every stage in its life (Hicks, 1973b, p. 13, 1973a, p. 100). Starting from period 0, as time goes by, it does not matter in which period the investor is standing, the NPV of the remaining periods should also be positive. Otherwise, the project would be liquidated at the first moment for which the NPV is negative. For the investor, the decision period is not just the initial one, every period is a decision period in which the investor looks again at the NPV and decides whether to continue with the project or to liquidate it. As the investor moves from period to period and expected and uncertain future conditions become known, the NPV may change from positive (negative) to negative (positive). Therefore, a project may have a shorter (longer) life than the one envisioned at its conception in period 0. Note, in connection with the discussion of the ABCT (Chapter 5 and Chapter 11), that the NPV of a project can change not only because the expected cash flow changes with updated information with the passing of time, but also with changes in the discount rate that can be subject to movements originating with monetary policy. Certainly, the concept, and uses of NPV are well known. Hicks's interesting angle is to point out how NPV (and thus perceptions of it) can change, for different reasons, over the life of the project.

A simple financial formalization

Let a_t and b_t be the value of inputs and outputs respectively in period t, where $a_t = \sum_i w_{it}\alpha_{it}$ and $b_t = \sum_j p_{jt}\beta_{jt}$. Variables w and α represent the prices and quantities of inputs respectively. Variables p and β represent the prices and quantities of outputs respectively. There are $i = 1,\ldots,m$ types of inputs and $j = 1,\ldots,\varphi$ types of output or final goods.

Let π be the *net output value* of the firm, such that for any period s, $\pi_t = b_t - a_t$. This is equivalent to the *accounting* profit of the firm. The opportunity cost of using capital goods owned by the firm (rather than renting) should also be taken into consideration, as should taxes.[4] In equilibrium, the economic profit of the firm will be zero. But, in the dynamic real world, where equilibrium is not present, the entrepreneur is seeking, and comparing alternative profit opportunities. The calculated capital-value (k) at any period t is the present value of future expected profits (Equation 8.1).

$$k_t = E_t[\pi_t]f^0 + E_t[\pi_{t+1}]f^1 + \cdots + E_t[\pi_n]f^n = \sum_t^{n-t}\frac{E_t[\pi_t]}{(1+r)^t} = \sum_t^n f^t E_t[\pi_t] \qquad 8.1$$

Where $f = \dfrac{1}{1+r}$ represents the discount factor and r represents the discount rate. Equation 8.1 is a well-known discounted cash flow. We can rewrite this expression as shown in Equation 8.2.

$$k_t = \pi_t + fk_{t+1} = (b_t - a_t) + fk_{t+1} \qquad 8.2$$

This is a simple transformation that shows that, for any period, the spot value of capital equals the current period *net output value* plus the present value of the remaining *net output values* over the rest of the life of the project. Hicks uses this representation to present his "Fundamental Theorem," according to which *it is always true that a fall in the rate of interest (rate of discount) will raise the capital-value of any project throughout (that is as calculated at any date t), while a rise will lower it*. Yet, Hicks's point is not just that a fall in r increases the value of k. Furthermore, he argues that as a fall in r makes

4 Interest payment on debt should not be counted if the objective is to see whether the profits earned will more than cover the "cost of capital." If they are counted, the rate of return must be interpreted as a premium rate in excess of the cost of borrowing.

future values of k_t rise and become positive, the *duration* of the project will be lengthened (or remain the same, but not contract). Duration and discount rate are negatively related: a fall in the latter *can* produce an increase in the former (if duration is allowed to vary – see his explanation in Hicks 1973a, pp. 20–21). Certainly, the value of k depends on a and b (meaning their respective sub-components) as well. Yet, Hicks shows an interest in the role that r and time (in the form of duration) have in the production process. This is Böhm-Bawerk's insight that he tried to save from his APP formulation.

There is also an important meaning attached to the internal rate of return (IRR). The IRR, also called the yield of the project, is the discount rate that makes the present value of its cash flow equal to the market price of the capital. Therefore, the IRR represents the minimum rate of return that the investor will ask from a project; otherwise, he will allocate his resources to some other project.

One can see a tradeoff between r and w, in the sense that a change in one can be compensated by changes in the other such that the value of k_0 remains unchanged. This represents a neo-Ricardian factor price frontier. There are different equilibria with a different income distribution. It is possible, then, to imagine how different production *techniques* can become dominant at different values of r. This is the basis of the reswitching problem. Yet, it should be taken into consideration that in principle, any pattern of α_t and β_t is possible. Therefore, there is no objective way to decide which project is more "capital intensive" in the typical neoclassical definition (also see Chapter 9).[5]

We need to repeat and emphasize another important point. In the *context* in which this discussion is taking place, r is not the price of capital (goods), it is the discount rate (the price of time) applied to *all* earnings captured in the cash flow. It is inside w where payments for labor, other services, and also rentals of capital goods, is included.

Looking forward and looking backward

Our previous discussion assumes the investor is *forward looking* and is estimating future cash flows, meaning that he is not looking at what *happened*, but looking at what is *expected* to happen. With more or less emphasis, there is always a speculative element to capital valuation. Yet, it is also possible to consider a *backward-looking* perspective on capital valuation (this is closer to Böhm-Bawerk's presentation) as shown in Equation 8.4 (assuming $k_0 = 0$ and dropping the expectation operator for simplicity).

5 We offer a more detailed discussion of this in Lewin and Cachanosky (2019 Appendix).

$$k_0 = \pi_0 + f^1\pi_1 + \cdots + f^t k_t \qquad 8.3$$

$$k_t = (-\pi_0) f^{-t} + (-\pi_1) f^{-(t-1)} + \cdots + (-\pi_{t-1}) f^{-1} \qquad 8.4$$

This equation states that the spot value of a capital good is the present value of its *past* associated net inputs $\pi_t = b_t - a_t$. Put differently, the equation is assuming that net inputs mature at the IRR rate until they emerge as consumption goods. This is similar to Hayek's triangular exposition.

In equilibrium, where expectations of the future value of π turn out to be correct, the *retrospective* (accumulated) and the *prospective* (discounted) valuation of capital are equivalent. In equilibrium, the valuation of capital is capturing an ongoing yet unchanging situation. Therefore, looking forward, or looking backward makes no difference. Hicks (1973a, p. 109) is skeptical of the importance attached to a steady-state equilibrium like this, since the "real world (perhaps fortunately) is not, and never is, in a steady-state ... A 'steady-state' theory is out of time; but an Austrian theory is in time." For a theory to be in time means that a *retrospective* and *prospective* view yield different results (history matters). For instance, any process with a rate of return higher than the market rate of interest (opportunity cost) will have a higher capital-value on its *prospective* than on its *retrospective* valuation, at *any* point in time. Profits (and losses) are a sign of disequilibrium.

This is one of the reasons why economic accounting seems to require the assumption that the market is in a steady-state. It is not possible to arrive at a time-consistent measure of the value of capital and output out of the steady-state. There is no single value of these variables out of equilibrium. For instance, this is why the choosing of a base year for economic indicators should pick one of a healthy and well-functioning economy, where market prices are expected to be closer to their equilibrium value than those of a crisis year.

Hicks's treatment is a more general, yet consistent, exposition than those of Böhm-Bawerk, Hayek, and Lachmann. For all these authors, including Hicks, capital has to be thought in terms of intertemporal plans. Capital appreciation and depreciation is the outcome of plans not matching the expectations of the investor (either because of a miscalculation or because of a change in consumers' valuation of final goods). Hicks's discussion also embodies the distinction between capital as factors of production and capital as value concept. Capital goods (as other factors of production), can be thought as "unfinished plans" and, therefore, said capital goods are valued by what they are expected to add to the value of the whole plan (Kirzner, 2010, Chapter 1).

Table 7.1 Böhm-Bawerk's APP and Hicks's AP

Böhm-Bawerk's APP – labor-input weights	*Hicks's AP (Macaulay's D) – present-value (output) weights*
$\sum_{t}^{n-t}\left[\underbrace{\frac{l_t}{\sum_t^{n-t} l_t}}_{weight}\cdot\underbrace{(n-t)}_{time}\right]$	$\sum_{t}^{n-t}\left[\underbrace{\frac{f^t\pi_t}{\sum_t^{n-t} f^t\pi_t}}_{weight}\cdot\underbrace{(t)}_{time}\right]$

The connection between capital and interest rates should be clear. Since the value of capital depends on the discount rate used, changes in the discount rate affect the valuation of factors of production and how they are seen to fit in different projects. This also means that the value of already existing plans will be affected. As suggested by the ABCT, and following the previous discussion by Hicks on interest rates and duration, a fall in discount rates leads to adopting *longer* projects. To be sure, the discount rate is but one of the variables that affect capital valuation. Yet, Hicks offers a financial framework that allows us to separate the effect of different variables on capital. We expand this financial framework in the next section of this book.

We finish this chapter with a comparison between Böhm-Bawerk's APP and Hicks's AP, which shows the validity of Hicks's argument that the latter more accurately and defensibly captures the spirit of what Böhm-Bawerk was trying to convey. As explained earlier the APP is a physical measure of time in terms of inputs like labor-hours. It is a cost production measure that has validity, if ever, only in an equilibrium steady-state economy where retrospective and prospective values are equivalent. By contrast, Hicks's AP is an output value measure that is valid for all situations, even though it does not yield a constant, objective measure of average production time – as no such measure exists. Hicks's AP (aka, the Macaulay duration), is the length of a project measured as the average amount of time for which one has to wait for $1. Duration is the weighted number of "periods" involved in a cash flow, where each period is weighted by the dollar amount (value) of their corresponding cash flows (see Chapters 1 and 2). Yet, despite the crucial difference between Böhm-Bawerk's physical approach to APP and Hicks's value definition of AP, some commonalities still exist. In fact, the formulas look very similar (Table 7.1).

There are two important differences between these formulations. The first one, already mentioned, is that Böhm-Bawerk is looking at a physical variable while Hicks is looking at market values.[6] The second is that Böhm-Bawerk's is *looking backward* while Hicks is *looking forward*. Böhm-Bawerk is looking at the contribution of past "stages of production" (as in Hayek), while Hicks is looking at the remaining time of the expected cash flows. As discussed above, Böhm-Bawerk, and Hicks's formulas are almost equivalent in the particular case of equilibrium. Crucially, they differ in an out-of-equilibrium dynamic economy.

6 It is true that there is an interpretation of Böhm-Bawerk's APP that renders it a kind of value measure. Ironically this is in terms of the labor theory of value, created by Ricardo, but fundamental to the Marxist view of the world that Böhm-Bawerk, in other works (1949), so effectively debunked. If one believes that the value of the output is determined by the accumulated value of the inputs (and not the other way around), then the "amount" of labor-hours embedded in the production of any output determines its "value." Then the APP is actually a measure of duration, accumulating value, from the past to the present, rather than discounting value, from the future to the present. But, as discussed above, the equivalence is not exact, because the APP in the above formula uses simple interest. Slightly modified to include compound interest, the equivalence is exact.

Part III

Financial applications

In Part III we apply the financial framework considered in the last chapter to a number of specific real-world economic issues. To do so, we add another concept from the field of finance, namely, EVA (economic value added). In the next chapter we derive the EVA from the familiar FCF analysis, which is equivalent to the simple Hicksian framework of the last chapter. In the subsequent chapters we apply an EVA analysis to various contexts including exchange rate fluctuations, Cantillon effects, managerial calculation, business cycles, and social institutions.

Chapter 8

The EVA® framework

From free cash flow (FCF) to economic value added (EVA®) – separating profit and loss results from investment decisions

As repeatedly discussed, the value of a capital good (or a firm), is the present value of its cash flow, sometimes known more specifically in the literature as its free cash flow (FCF). Notwithstanding the benefits and widespread use of the FCF approach, there is one particular shortcoming that can make it difficult to easily assess the financial soundness of a firm. In particular, *the FCF methodology mixes business-operation results (profits and losses) with investment decisions (i.e., changes in the quantities of capital goods and raw materials).* It is possible, for example, that a firm making profits over a particular period is also financing a large investment and, as a result, its FCF will have a negative value. In other words, a negative FCF in any given period could be either because the firm is making losses or because it is making an investment larger than the profit of the period. The EVA transformation that we discuss in this chapter (and use in the following ones) offers two advantages. One is to separate business-operation results from investment decisions and to observe if, despite a large investment, the firm is actually making profits over any given period. The second one is to offer a more economically friendly presentation.

Let us first introduce some terminology. We will relate the concepts commonly used in this literature to those discussed in this book. In this chapter in particular, we note the distinction between two kinds of expenditures (accounting costs), those resources used for the production of current output (sold for current revenue) and those resources used to add to the production of future output (to be sold for future revenue).

- FCF_t = the free-cash-flow in the period $t = \pi_t = b_t - a_t$. As previously explained, π_t is equivalent to the *accounting* profit of the firm, where a_t

and b_t are the values of inputs and outputs respectively in the period t.[1] (For simplicity, we assume there are no taxes. If there were, they would be counted as a cost)

- $NI_t = W_t - W_{t-1}$ is the net investment in period t, where $W_t = W_0 + \sum_1^t NI_t$
- $NOPAT_t =$ the net operating profits after taxes, which corresponds to the *net output value* of the firm, such that for any period t, it is equal to $\pi_t - NI_t = b_t - a_t - (W_t - W_{t-1})$
- $ROIC_t$ = the current "return on invested capital" $\left(\frac{NOPAT_t}{K_0 + \sum_1^t NI_t}\right) = \left(\frac{NOPAT_t}{W_t}\right)$
- c = the weighted average cost of capital ($WACC$) over the relevant period
- EVA_t = the economic value added of any given period equals the spread between the $ROIC$ and c times accumulated investments (W_t).
- MVA_t = the market value added up to the end of period t = $\sum_{t=1}^{\infty} f^t EVA_t$

  where, it will be remembered $f^t = \frac{1}{(1+c)^t}$ is the discount factor

There is a notation clarification to be made. In the EVA and financial literature, it is typical to use the letter K instead of W. We use W to avoid a potential confusion. In this work, we refer to K as the present value of the services provided by productive assets. In the EVA literature, K represents the amount of money an investor is adding (subtracting) from a firm. A confusion may arise, for instance, because now the variable K would be on the other side of the present-value equation.[2]

There is another clarification to be made. The EVA methodology we develop below is a management tool, and as such requires a set of judgment calls by the entrepreneur. For instance, an expenditure in a marketing campaign can either be considered an operating cost of the firm or an investment that is

1 Remember, form the previous chapter, $a_t = \sum_i w_{it} \alpha_{it}$ and $b_t = \sum_j p_{jt} \beta_{jt}$. Variables w and α represent the prices and quantities of inputs respectively. Variables p and β represent the prices and quantities of outputs respectively. There are $i = 1, \dots, m$ types of inputs and $j = 1, \dots, \varphi$ types of output or final goods.

2 And, of course, as we have discussed, in the neoclassical literature K represents a "physical" factor of production.

expected to increase profits in the future. This decision expresses how profits are perceived by entrepreneurs, managers, investors, etc.[3] How the tool is to be applied to each particular case is a decision based on subjective judgment. This is another way to look at the intricacies of the maintenance of the capital of the firm as discussed earlier in Chapter 4.

The discussion below should not be understood as a description of an application that yields the objective true measure of the value of the firm. Value is subjective, and its estimation, even by a method that follows general rules of calculation, must rely on subjective assumptions and interpretations. This "internal" entrepreneurial assessment can affect how the profits of the firm are perceived.

This judgment component in valuing a firm has yet another implication. The assumptions of how to value a firm are also in themselves entrepreneurial decisions. The entrepreneur *qua* entrepreneur usually describes the act of finding profit opportunities (more on this in the next chapter) out there, as it were, in the market. Yet, the decision of whether to count an expenditure such as a marketing campaign as a necessary operating cost or as an investment in brand building, requires an entrepreneurial interpretation, and a decision within the firm. In this sense, entrepreneurs need not only apply their skills to the market, to spot profit opportunities, they also need to be entrepreneurs inside their own firm.

Then, using the above terminology, $FCF = NOPAT + NI$ and $EVA = (ROIC - c) \cdot W$ in any period (suppressing subscripts for simplicity). We can see now how it is possible that the FCF would be negative while the firm is experiencing a positive $NOPAT$, namely when $NOPAT > 0$ but $|-NI| > NOPAT$. If the (capital) value of the firm is represented by CV (and assuming a constant c for simplicity), then the Equations 8.1 and 8.2 are mathematically equivalent (see the Appendix for a derivation).[4]

$$CV_o = \sum_{t=0}^{\infty} f^t FCF_t \qquad 8.1$$

$$CV_0 = W_0 + \sum_{t=1}^{\infty} f^t \left(ROIC_t - c\right) W_{t-1} = W_0 + \sum_{t=1}^{\infty} f^t EVA_t = W_0 + MVA \qquad 8.2$$

3 That this is another way to look at the intricacies of the maintenance of the capital of the firm (as discussed above in Chapter 4) should be apparent.

4 For a more detailed discussion of the EVA methodology, especially with its applications to corporate finance, see Cachanosky, J.C. (1999), Ehrbar (1998), Koller, Goedhart, and Wessels (1990), Shiely and Ross (2003), and Young and O'Byrne (2000).

Note the following characteristics of the EVA representation (Equation 8.2). First, EVA is an attempt to capture the familiar concept of economic profit, as the return on invested funds minus its opportunity cost (c). It is a reflection of the net value expected to be added by the investment, regardless of the size of operating profit or loss. Net investment is captured as different values of W in each period. The value of the firm is represented as the initial value of W *plus* the present value of future expected $EVAs$, which equals the market value (to be) added (MVA) (that is, the market value[5] added to W_0).

A simple analogy may help. Consider two investors who are considering investing in the same project. For both of them, W_0 has the same value, which is the market price of the productive assets they need to acquire at the startup to run the business. However, their own subjective expectations of how well or badly the business would do in future periods means each one of them will "see" a different MVA. In other words, W_0 can also be read as the market value these investors would get today if they decided to sell their business to someone else, while MVA represents what they think they can add to the market value of the productive assets under their control (we will return to this in the next chapter). Note that this is also Mises's conception of capital as a financial construct rather than as physical goods.

The EVA framework is mostly applied in the world of corporate finance. As a corporate tool, it can be used to assess whether or not the firm is creating value and how different areas are performing (see the next section), to define market strategies, and even to develop compensation rules for managers. Of course, such application requires judgment and assumptions on the part of the managers (i.e., how to split operating costs and investments). Interestingly, a number of firms decide to base compensation strategies on EVA results as a way to solve the principal-agent problem. In short, managers are paid to produce more profits as measured by EVA rather than FCF or accounting profits. For outsiders, such as financial analysts, making an "EVA evaluation" of a firm can offer a clearer assessment of the firm's situation and allow one to decide if stock prices are accurately capturing the "fundamentals" of the firm depending upon one's assessment of the MVA.

We can illustrate the differences between FCF and EVA methodologies with a simple simulation (Table 8.1). Assume a firm has a forecast of four periods of growth. In period five the firm reaches a steady growth rate that can be represented as a perpetuity where the firm growth rate equals the opportunity cost of capital (from period 5 onwards, the firm's investment

5 It may help to remember that by "market value" we mean the price the entrepreneur imagines the firm would fetch in the market were it to be sold.

Table 8.1 Comparison of FCF and EVA methodologies

Period	*0*	*1*	*2*	*3*	*4*	*5*
Revenue	$1,000	$1,100	$1,200	$1,200	$1,600	$1,700
Costs	$600	$650	$700	$1,000	$1,000	$1,100
Profit	$400	$450	$500	$200	$600	$600
Taxes (10%)	$40	$45	$50	$20	$60	$60
NOPAT	$360	$405	$450	$180	$540	$540
Net Investment (*NI*)	$0	$100	$800	$600	$100	$0
Invested Funds (*W*)	$1,000	$1,000	$1,100	$1,900	$2,500	$2,600
ROIC (*NOPAT/W*)	0.36	0.41	0.41	0.09	0.22	0.21
Opportunity cost of capital (*c*)	0.10	0.10	0.10	0.10	0.10	0.10
FCF (*NOPAT – NI*)	$360	$305	-$350	-$420	$440	$5,400*
FCF (Present value)		$277	-$289	-$316	$301	$3,688*
Firm value (FCF methodology)	$3,661					
EVA	$260	$305	$340	-$10	$290	$2,800*
EVA (Present value)		$277	$281	-$8	$198	$1,912*
EVA (Sum of present value)	$2,661					
Initial capital	$1,000					
Firm value (EVA methodology)	$3,661					

* Denotes perpetuity value.

equals the cost of capital such that the capital stock remains constant).[6] Let the company invest to increase its future revenue and attempt to maximize its expected market value. In period one, the net investment is less than the NOPAT, and therefore the firm shows a positive FCF. However, in periods two and three the firm expects to increase its net investment, so the FCF is negative even if the NOPAT is positive. Yet, there is a difference between these two periods. In period two, we observe a positive EVA. However, in period three we observe a negative EVA, not because the firm has a negative NOPAT, but because the return on capital (ROIC) is less than its opportunity cost (c). In period four, the firm has positive accounting profits $(Profit > 0)$ but negative economic profits $(\text{EVA} < 0)$. Finally, let us assume that $c = 0.10$ and that $W_0 = \$1{,}000$.

6 For instance, the present value of the EVA in period five would be: $CV_0 = f^4 \cdot \frac{EVA_5}{c}$, where $f^4 = \frac{1}{(1+c)^4}$ is the discount factor in period 4.

Table 8.1 illustrates the above-discussed features of the EVA methodology. It represents what the entrepreneur of this project *thinks* is going to happen to his or her business under his or her managerial skills. Let us emphasize that the EVA representation is mathematically equivalent to the FCF calculation (that is why both methods yield the same firm value). The difference is in *how* information is presented and not in *what* is being calculated. EVA does not claim to have a different or better valuation result, rather it offers a potentially more transparent way to represent what is happening to the firm. For business managers, EVA offers better information in order to make better decisions based on the judgment of how to interpret different costs. Look, in particular, at period 2. A simple look at the FCF may suggest that the firm has incurred losses in that period. However, the EVA representation shows that the firm actually made $281 in profits in present-value terms. While both methodologies get to the same valuation of the overall performance of the firm, the EVA representation offers a more transparent reflection of *each* period that the firm is being evaluated. As mentioned above, we can see that the EVA framework also shows the evolution of the financial capital of the firm. Changes in the size of the firm (net investment) is not lost information, it is just represented from a different perspective.[7]

In terms of textbook microeconomic market equilibrium, in the long run, freedom of entry and exit in the market ceases when $EVA = 0$ for all firms. At this point, the owners of the firm receive a ROIC that just compensates for their opportunity cost. EVA, like standard economic profits, is a measure of *extra-ordinary* profits, or profits beyond the opportunity cost of capital. This would be the financial equivalent of long-run equilibrium under perfect competition.

Rather than a financial application to the world of business, we are interested in extending the EVA framework to the problems discussed in the previous chapters and to also offer some applications to other microeconomic issues, including business cycles and to capture some institutional issues (covered in the next chapters respectively). There are, however, other EVA features to discuss before extending its application to these economic problems.

A deeper look: value drivers

The EVA framework offers an overall assessment of the firm. Yet, an EVA calculation can also be disaggregated into its "value drivers." The value drivers are the micro-components of the firm that are expected to add to its value. This is done by disaggregating the NOPAT into different components.

7 This is the situation, for instance, of Amazon reporting negative profits for a number of years while investing heavily in the value of the firm. Uber is currently reporting huge losses and investors' assessent of its *CV* depends on their expected MVA or EVA in each period.

Let us multiply and divide the ROIC by total revenue (TR).[8] NOPAT equals total revenue minus the different costs that the firm incurs (such as depreciation, inventory maintenance, marketing, etc., captured as $C_1,\ldots,C_n$). For simplicity, we assume there are no taxes and therefore there is no need to make a tax adjustment. Then, we can rewrite Equation 8.3 as Equation 8.4 (time subscripts are suppressed for simplicity).

$$ROIC = \frac{NOPAT}{W} \tag{8.3}$$

$$ROIC = \frac{\frac{NOPAT}{TR} \times TR}{W}$$

$$ROIC = \frac{\frac{TR - C_1 - C_2 - \cdots - C_n}{TR} \times TR}{W}$$

$$ROIC = \left[\underbrace{1 - \frac{C_1}{TR} - \frac{C_2}{TR} - \cdots - \frac{C_n}{TR}}_{value\ drivers} \right] \cdot \frac{TR}{W} \tag{8.4}$$

Equation 8.4 represents the current return on capital (invested funds) as one minus the different costs of the firm (from one to n) as shares of the total revenue. These are the *value drivers*. Then, the value drivers are indexed by the accumulated investment funds up to each period of the firm to get the typical return over invested capital (ROIC) measure. What this expression does is to open the EVA, or more precisely, the ROIC, into its micro-components. For instance, a firm can observe that C_1 is a heavy drag on its ROIC and try to find a way to reduce the C_1/TR ratio, to attempt to increase ROIC, and with it the EVA. Alternatively, a firm may observe that C_2 has a small impact on the ROIC, and therefore not much energy should be allocated in trying to economize this type of cost in the firm.

The more disaggregated the value drivers are, the more accurate the information the firm can obtain on what is driving its returns. It is also possible to disaggregate total revenue into its own components (denoted by the Greek letter

8 In standard microeconomic analysis, $\pi = TR - TC$. So, $TR = a_t = \sum_i w_{it}\alpha_{it}$ and $TC = b_t = \sum_j p_{jt}\beta_{jt}$.

Ω). Consider Equations 8.5 and 8.6 (where $\omega_i = \Omega_i / TR$ and $\theta_i = C_i / TR$), which offer a more general representation of Equation 8.4.

$$ROIC = \left[\left(\frac{\Omega_1}{TR} + \frac{\Omega_2}{TR} + \dots + \frac{\Omega_m}{TR}\right) - \left(\frac{C_1}{TR} + \frac{C_2}{TR} + \dots + \frac{C_n}{TR}\right)\right] \cdot \frac{TR}{W} \qquad 8.5$$

$$ROIC = \left[(\omega_1 + \omega_2 + \dots + \omega_m) - (\theta_1 + \theta_2 + \dots + \theta_n)\right] \cdot \frac{TR}{W} \qquad 8.6$$

In this representation, each © can represent a different geographic area where the firm operates, or a different business unit, or maybe a different product family, etc. Consider a large car manufacturer. The value drivers can be represented by country (United States, Canada, etc.), or by type of client (private consumer, corporate, etc.), or also by type of car (sedans, trucks, sport cars, etc.) Similarly, there can be different ways to slice the operating costs of the firm. It is also possible to disaggregate W into different components, and evaluate the return on the investment structure of the firm, or by type of investor, or geographic location of the investor, etc. A value-driver analysis can be adapted to the different needs and concerns of the firm managers.

If a slice of revenue (ω) is matched with its slice of costs (θ), then we can see the economic profit or loss per "slice" of the firm. This matching shows if the return of any of these slices is more or less than its associated opportunity cost. Certainly, a perfect matching may not be possible, as some costs are shared by different areas of the firm (e.g., depreciation on a shared manufacturing plant), among a number of other overlapping cash flows. Yet, this principle can guide the manager's *eva*luation of the firm to provide a more precise, if not perfect, map of sources of profit.[9]

From a corporate-finance point of view, value drivers allow a close inspection of the source of economic profit (that is, EVAs) of the firm. From an economic analysis point of view, it also allows one to track how relative price distortions can affect management decisions given their choice of how to categorize different costs. If certain policies affect relative

9 This is perhaps as close as one can come to "imputing" the value of the firm's output to various inputs, thus providing a "pragmatic" solution to the so-called "imputation problem."

prices in a certain way, then the value drivers of the firm will change and therefore managerial decisions can be affected (more on this in the next chapter). Economically speaking, this can lead to a misallocation of resources, overinvestment, and a number of problems that for the firm would appear like sound decisions given the prices they observe (more on this in Chapters 10 and 11).

This discussion is not meant to imply that the firm should not also consider what the optimal capital size of the capital structure is for the firm. Namely, managers should also worry about what size of W maximizes the MVA and what impact the financial structure of K may have on the value of the firm.

Equation 8.2 shows that an increase in W would increase the EVA by the marginal effect of the invested funds on the NOPAT and reduce it by the opportunity cost of capital. As long as output faces diminishing marginal returns, there is a point where the net effect of an increase in W produces a fall in EVA.[10] In addition, even if the size of W remains constant, the firm may change its structure in a way that reduces c (especially if there are financial frictions). For instance, besides the tax-shield effect, debt as a source of capital is less risky than equity, and therefore a lower capital charge is used. At which point and when these effects happen is also dependent on how the entrepreneur sees the project, i.e., what is an investment, and what is a cost of operation.

If we place Equation 8.6 into Equation 8.2, we get a more detailed calculation of the firm value in terms of the value drivers. As Equation 8.7 shows, now the ROIC component of the value of the firm is disaggregated into its own drivers, offering a more detailed analysis of where the economic profits of the firm are coming from.

$$CV_0 = W_0 + \sum_{t=1}^{\infty} f^t \left[((\omega_1 + \dots + \omega_m) - (\theta_1 + \dots + \theta_n)) \cdot \frac{TR}{W_{t-1}} - c \right] W_{t-1} \qquad 8.7$$

10 Note that $EVA = \left(\frac{NOPAT(K)}{W} - c \right) K = NOPAT(K) - cW$. Then, $\frac{\partial EVA}{\partial W} = \frac{\partial NOPAT(W)}{\partial W} - c$. EVA increases with more capital if $\frac{\partial NOPAT(W)}{\partial W} > c$. However, if there are diminishing marginal returns to capital, then $\frac{\partial^2 NOPAT(W)}{\partial W^2} < 0$.

What is capital intensity?

Since Böhm-Bawerk's introduction of *roundaboutness*, the problem of period of production and capital intensity has been vigorously debated. We have already covered some of these issues in more detail in previous chapters. Yet, there is still another dimension of *roundaboutness* that the EVA framework helps to clarify. That is the issue of capital intensity.

One of the reasons the concept of *roundaboutness* is so elusive and open to dispute is that it conflates two of the dimensions of capital with the third dimension – time and quantity with value. Böhm-Bawerk's intuition is that a lower interest rate will be associated with longer periods of production. In financial terms, a lower discount rate is associated with investments that exhibit a higher duration – the time dimension. The quantity dimension is expressed as (physical) capital intensity. It is often suggested that Böhm-Bawerk may be interpreted to say that a lower interest rate is associated with a higher capital intensity and this is how his work has been incorporated into formal mainstream economics. In principle, one can imagine that one of these two dimensions increases while the other decreases, or that they move independently. For instance, a firm may decide to extend its production process in time by employing more labor rather than capital goods. This may be because the decision of how to combine different productive assets is constrained by their heterogeneity. The issue of how these two dimensions interact, and if they are correlated, when discount rates change, is not a simple one.

In particular, the issue of capital intensity has been a focus of debate in the capital controversies and it has been suggested that the problem of "reswitching" is a serious shortcoming in neoclassical production theory. If the interest rate is the price of capital, and capital intensity reswitches (changes direction at least twice) with a unidirectional movement of its price (thought to be the interest rate), then capital goods cannot be assumed to have a well-behaved demand function. This problem is usually represented in the following format. Assume two production technologies with the same constant labor input but different amounts of physical capital. As the discount rate decreases, the more capital intensive technology is adopted for the less capital intensive technology; only to then be changed once back again to the more capital-intensive technology as the interest rate continues to fall.[11] This is sometimes presented as a "paradox." The paradox would be the reswitching

11 This is a simplified and inaccurate way of stating the claim. More precisely, the comparative equilibrium rankings of alternative production techniques according to capital-intensity will switch and reswitch. What this says about real world disequilibrium production decisions is not at all clear, but the protagonists in the debate regarded this phenomenon as fatal to the idea of capital as a physical factor of production earning a marginal product. For a more detailed discussion on the problem of reswitching see Cohen and Harcourt (2003), Lewin and Cachanosky (2019 appendix), and Osborne and Davidson (2016).

in the use of capital as its price moves sequentially in the same direction. Algebraically, or financially, this is hardly a paradox. The present value of a cash flow is a polynomial equation of degree n (number of periods) with n roots. These roots (in financial terms the internal rate of return or the IRR) are the "points" where capital intensity would switch.

There are two reasons why the reswitching objections do not affect our approach to capital theory. The first one is that the reswitching debate is framed in terms of capital as goods rather than as a financial value. In the typical neoclassical framework, capital intensity is to be understood as capital goods per unit of labor, K / L.

However, as emphasized in this book K does *not* represent physical tools, rather it represents a financial construct, the value of *all* productive assets regardless of their physical form. Thus, the financial capital-value of a firm includes tools, but it also includes the value of labor and other productive assets. In financial terms, the question is not whether a reduction in the discount rate leads to the use of more or less physical capital, but whether it leads to the use of more or less productive assets of any form. Since productive assets are heterogeneous, they can only be aggregated in monetary terms, namely, financial capital.

The second reason why the reswitching objections do not affect our approach is because we consider the interest rate to be the price of time (credit), not the price of capital. The price of a tool is, like any other price, the amount we have to pay to *buy* said tool. Reswitching would be a more serious issue if, *ceteris paribus*, the quantity demanded reswitched as the price to *buy* the capital good (or its services) decreased. If the price of a tool was to be considered a market price rather than the interest rate, such as the wage for labor services, then there would be no reswitching concerns, just as there is no labor-price (wage) reswitching problem.

If the interest rate is considered to be the price of capital, then an unacceptable circular reference would be involved. The price of a capital good is the present value of its output, but to get the present value the output has to be discounted by this price. The logic in thinking that the interest rate = the discount rate = the price of capital, is seriously problematic.

This inconsistency is not an issue if the interest rate is understood to be the price of time instead of the price of capital. The interest rate as the price of time is the topic discussed in Part I of this book. The entrepreneurial concern is whether all productive assets can yield between today and tomorrow a return above its opportunity cost (the interest rate). Intuitively, a discounted cash flow compares the value generated by the project with the value of the best alternative foregone.

We may ask then, following our arguments that capital should be understood as a financial construct rather than as a physical aggregate, what is capital intensity? How should K / L be interpreted? The EVA representation suggests that if anything is going to be understood by capital intensity this is not the typical representation K / L (tools per unit of labor). Rather, it should be understood in terms of how much funding the firm is using (W). Admittedly, there is no "intensity" in this variable, but there is no need to consider this problematic. The value of W may be more relevant than the ratio of two different productive assets (two different types of capital goods). How are capital goods per unit of labor more relevant than, say, the quantity of machines type 1 over quantity of machines type 2? To arrive at a capital intensity measure, we need to designate *some* of all productive assets as capital. This partial (and arbitrary) look at K will, of course, result in "non-normal behaviors" such as the reswitching problem. We are afraid that the physical conception of capital, and the focus on capital intensity, may have channeled too much energy into issues that are not as relevant as they seem and that ultimately depend significantly on definitions and semantics (Lewin & Cachanosky, 2018a).

The analogous question to that of "what happens to capital intensity when there is a change in the discount rate?" would be "what happens to the funds investors inject in a firm when there is a change in the discount rate?" Is the present value of projects that use more funds more sensitive to changes in the discount rate than projects that require less funds? In other words, is there a duration relationship with respect to the size of W?

Duration, time, capital, and W

The general principle presented in this book, that the average period of production should be understood as the Macaulay duration of the project's cash flow, remains intact in the EVA framework. All that happens is that *how* the information is shown is changed, not the principle behind it. Consider Equations 8.8 and 8.9, which show the Macaulay duration of an EVA cash flow.

$$D = \frac{\sum_{t=1}^{T\to\infty} f^t \cdot (EVA_t \cdot t)}{\sum_{t=1}^{T\to\infty} f^t \cdot EVA_t} = \frac{\sum_{t=1}^{T\to\infty} f^t \cdot (EVA_t \cdot t)}{MVA} \qquad 8.8$$

$$D = \frac{\sum_{t=1}^{T\to\infty} f^t \cdot \left((ROIC_t - c)W_{t-1}t\right)}{\sum_{t=1}^{T\to\infty} f^t \cdot (ROIC_t - c)W_{t-1}} = \frac{\sum_{t=1}^{T\to\infty} f^t \cdot \left((ROIC_t - c)W_{t-1}t\right)}{MVA} \qquad 8.9$$

Note, first, that even if the cash flow is assumed to have infinite periods, D is still a finite number $(D < \infty)$. This is because the denominator grows exponentially. In a typical economic context, where the numerator is subject to diminishing marginal returns on the factors of production (or constant returns to scale), it is unlikely that it will follow an explosive path as the denominator does. Therefore, even if we are a facing *forward-looking* cash flow with an infinite horizon, the *APP* is still finite. This contrasts with the *backward-looking* approach to measuring the period of production, where the initial period of the *APP* has to be chosen arbitrarily or else one has to contemplate an infinite past period of time.[12]

The perspective we offer here characterizes investments not simply according to the *quantity* of capital involved, which, as we have shown is a highly ambiguous concept, but rather according to the capital-value (*CV*) and the duration (*D*) of the investment. *D* captures the magnitude of *waiting* that is involved (on average) and, for this reason, is also an aspect of how risky the investment is, while the *CV* captures its *size*. A third consideration is its profitability (internal rate of return). The entrepreneur must weigh up these variables in deciding on investments. The more profitable an investment seems, other things equal, the more likely an entrepreneur is to wait for the payoff. The size of the W_t, the accumulated investments, in itself, does not have the value of the "capital" of the business, but rather is an indication of how much investment will be required under the plan as reflected by the projected earnings.

From a macroeconomic perspective, to which we turn in Chapter 10, the EVA framework isolates how the investment structure of the firm might be affected by a monetary policy that, for example, changes the cost of borrowing in financial markets, *c*. By reducing the opportunity cost of investing, such a policy could produce investments that appear profitable to the entrepreneur, but, turn out not to be, this contributing to a credit-induced business cycle. This adds valuable microeconomic detail to business-cycle theory (see Lewin, 2018) on the absence of sufficient microfoundations in ABCT).

These considerations bear, once again, on the question of the amount of capital contained in a project or a technique of production, which was the target of the attack by the Cambridge neo-Ricardians against neoclassical capital theory. We show here, once again, that while it is possible to construct irregular cash flows that may defy some of the expected outcomes, the pattern result is that, in the sense explained, both more time and "more capital" are associated with a higher duration, which has the dual interpretation of being a measure of the average period of production and also a measure of the sensitivity of value to the discount rate (see Osborne & Davidson, 2016).

Appendix: the EVA® derivation[13]

To go from the FCF representation to its EVA equivalent we need to pull out the net investment (NI) from the FCF and rewrite it as changes in financial

12 This was another issue raised in the capital controversies.

13 See Cachanosky and Lewin (2014, p. 663) and Koller, Goedhart, and Wessels (1990 Appendix B).

capital. Recall that $FCF = NOPAT - NI$. Assuming, again, a constant c for simplicity. Following Koller, Goedhart, and Wessels (1990, Appendix B):

$$CV_0 = \sum_{t=0}^{\infty} f^t \cdot FCF_t$$

$$CV_0 = \sum_{t=0}^{\infty} f^t \cdot W_t - \sum_{t=0}^{\infty} f^t \cdot W_t + \sum_{t=0}^{\infty} f^t \cdot FCF_t$$

$$CV_0 = W_0 + \sum_{t=0}^{\infty} f^t \cdot W_t - \sum_{t=1}^{\infty} f^{t-1} \cdot W_{t-1} + \sum_{t=0}^{\infty} f^t \cdot FCF_t$$

$$CV_0 = W_0 + \sum_{t=1}^{\infty} f^t \cdot W_t - \sum_{t=1}^{\infty} f^t \cdot (1-c) W_{t-1} + \sum_{t=0}^{\infty} f^t \cdot NOPAT_t - NI_t$$

$$CV_0 = W_0 + \sum_{t=1}^{\infty} f^t \cdot (W_t - (1+c) W_{t-1} + NOPAT_t - (W_t - W_{t-1}))$$

$$CV_0 = W_0 + \sum_{t=1}^{\infty} f^t \cdot (-W_{t-1} - cW_{t-1} + NOPAT_t + W_{t-1})$$

$$CV_0 = W_0 + \sum_{t=1}^{\infty} f^t \cdot (NOPAT_t - cW_{t-1})$$

$$CV_0 = W_0 + \sum_{t=1}^{\infty} f^t \cdot \left[\left(\frac{NOPAT_t}{W_{t-1}} - c \right) W_{t-1} \right]$$

$$CV_0 = W_0 + \sum_{t=1}^{\infty} f^t \cdot EVA_t = W_0 + MVA$$

Chapter 9

EVA and microeconomics

One of the advantages of the financial approach to capital theory is that it offers the opportunity to develop an analysis based on how the entrepreneur *actually* makes decisions rather than being based on an "as if" scenario. If we imagine investment decisions are made by looking at the present value of expected cash flows, we have the foundations to track down economic behavior to financial changes.

In particular, the value drivers discussed in the previous chapter prove to be useful. Value drivers disaggregate profits into prices making a relative-price analysis possible. In this sense, the EVA treatment previously discussed offers a roadmap to develop financial microfoundations. These financial microfoundations can be applied to macroeconomic problems as well (next chapter).

A financial look at economics offers other applications as well. We cover three of those in this chapter. The first one relates to the role of exchange rates in international trade. The second incorporates Cantillon effects into the EVA framework. Finally, the third one, covers the problem of economic calculation under socialism.

Relative prices and economic profit in the EVA framework

In conventional microeconomics, the profit (π) of the firm is represented as total revenue minus total costs. There is no time consideration, therefore there is no need to discount the economic profit of different periods to its present value. It is also usual to divide total costs into two components, labor (L) and capital (with the usual K). Labor is measured in labor units (i.e., hours of work) and multiplied by the wage per unit (w). Capital shows up differently. Capital is already a nominal value that is multiplied by the interest rate (r), which is interpreted to be its price.[1] This is shown in the familiar Equation 8.7 (where $\boldsymbol{p}$ and $\boldsymbol{q}$ are the price and quantity vectors respectively).

$$\pi = \boldsymbol{pq} - wL - rK \qquad 9.1$$

More generally and more informatively we can write

$$\pi = \boldsymbol{pq} - \boldsymbol{wL} - \boldsymbol{rK} \qquad 9.1$$

where all the variables on the right-hand side are vectors, in other words, there are multiple types of output, labor, and capital goods.

We also know that EVA is the financial equivalent of economic profits. Therefore, we can represent the value of the firm by inserting Equation 9.1 into the EVA framework. We can easily see the relation of ROIC to π by dividing the latter by K (Equation 9.2 where bold letters represent vectors). If L represents the services of *all factors of production*, and if $r = c$, then $\frac{\pi}{K}$ is equivalent to $ROIC$. Recall, that this financial K is the amount of dollars allocated by the investor rather than the present value of a cash flow. For the reasons discussed in the previous chapter, we use W instead of K.[2]

$$\frac{\pi}{W} = \frac{\boldsymbol{pq} - \boldsymbol{wL}}{W} - r \qquad 9.2$$

Use now Equation 9.2 as ROIC in the EVA framework. Assume the firm produces n goods and uses m factors of production. Then, Equation 8.7 becomes 9.3.

$$CV = W_0 + \sum_{t=1}^{\infty} f^t \left(\frac{\sum_{i=1}^{n} p_{i,t} q_{i,t} - \sum_{j=1}^{m} w_{j,t} L_{j,t}}{W_{t-1}} - c \right) W_{t-1} \qquad 9.3$$

1 This is an example of what Fisher (2005) calls "quantities measured in value terms" that renders the use and meaning of K so problematic.

2 The firm also presents the issue of the dual meaning of K. Assume a typical Cobb-Douglas function, $q = A \cdot K^{\alpha} L^{1-\alpha}$ where A is total factor productivity, K is physical capital, L is labor, and $\alpha \in (0,1)$ is the output elasticity of the factor of production. Now replace q in the firm's profit formula: $\pi = p \cdot (A \cdot K^{\alpha} L^{1-\alpha}) - wL - rK$. In the *same* formula we have K that represents physical goods (in the first term) and a nominal value (in the last term). No wonder that "capital" is a term surrounded by much ambiguity and confusion.

If we expand ROIC to reveal its value drivers, then it is easy to see how changes in relative prices will affect how profits are seen by the entrepreneur (Equation 9.4, where $\omega_i = q_i p_i$ and $\theta_j = w_j L_j$)

$$CV_0 = W_0 + \sum_{t=1}^{\infty} f^t \left[\frac{\sum_{i=1}^{n} p_{i,t} q_{i,t} - \sum_{j=1}^{m} w_{j,t} L_{j,t}}{\boldsymbol{p_t q_t}} \cdot \frac{\boldsymbol{p_t q_t}}{W_{t-1}} - c \right] W_{t-1}$$

$$CV_0 = W_0 + \sum_{t=1}^{\infty} f^t \left[\left(\left(\omega_{1,t} + \cdots + \omega_{n,t} \right) - \left(\theta_{1,t} + \cdots + \theta_{m,t} \right) \right) \cdot \frac{\boldsymbol{p_t q_t}}{W_{t-1}} - c \right] W_{t-1} \quad 9.4$$

As long as changes in relative prices change the value drivers, then profit opportunities as perceived by the entrepreneurs will change as well. Resources will be reallocated from goods with low value creation toward goods with high value creation. Note that this resource reallocation can occur even if total profit does not change as long as its value drivers do. For instance, ω_1 may decrease and ω_2 may increase in a way such that ROIC remains unaffected.

It follows that shifts in demand and supply will be captured in changes in the value drivers. In simple terms, we may say that a shift in demand changes an ω value (e.g., a change in population, preferences, etc.) while a shift in supply would affect a θ value (i.e., change in wages, new technologies, etc.) To be able to discover new profit opportunities, entrepreneurs need to apply their judgment in two areas. The first one is to decide what constitutes a cost of operation and what constitutes an investment for a firm and industry. The second is to know how to define and slice the different value drivers and how much of a shared cost should be assigned to each "value-driver slice."

International trade

We can use exchange rates as an example of the effects of price movements in the perceived profits of the entrepreneur. Let us assume a firm that produces two different goods, one for the domestic market (DM) and another one for the international sector (I). Further, let us assume that all factors of production are hired in the domestic market. Finally, let e denote the nominal exchange rate. Then, Equations 9.3 and 9.4 become Equations 9.5 and 9.6.

$$CV_0 = W_0 + \sum_{t=1}^{\infty} f^t \left[\frac{p_{DM,t} q_{DM,t} + e_t p_{I,t} \cdot q_{I,t} - \boldsymbol{w_t L_t}}{p_{DM,t} q_{DM,t} + e_t \cdot p_{I,t} q_{I,t}} \cdot \right. \quad 9.5$$

$$\left. \frac{p_{DM,t} q_{D,t} + e_t p_{I,t} \cdot q_{I,t}}{W_{t-1}} - c \right] W_{t-1}$$

$$CV_0 = W_0 + \sum_{t=1}^{\infty} f^t \left[\left(\left(\omega_{DM,t} + \omega_{I,t} \right) - \theta_t \right) \cdot \frac{p_{DM,t} q_{DM,t} + e_t p_{I,t} \cdot q_{I,t}}{W_{t-1}} - c \right] W_{t-1} \qquad 9.6$$

For this firm, a movement in the nominal exchange rate changes the weight of the domestic and international value drivers. Since this firm is in the export business, a depreciation (appreciation) of the domestic currency increases (decreases) the economic value added of the export good. The opposite effect would be for a firm that sells domestically but needs to import some of its factors of production.

An exchange rate policy based on keeping the nominal exchange rate depreciated to favor exports will, as expected, trigger a reallocation of resources from domestic to international production. In addition, exchange rate volatility would increase the standard deviation of ω_I which, as a risk measure, would reduce the resource allocation in the export sector. To deal with the exchange rate risk, we can envision that the firm decides to cover the exchange rate risk with future forward exchange-rate contracts, so e becomes fixed and the cost of the financial hedging would be captured as an increase in θ.

Certainly, this is a very simple exposition. A number of issues and complications in international trade can also be discussed. However, this example is just intended to show a simple example of how the general EVA representation at the microlevel (value drivers) can be accommodated to capture effects of interest. In this case, the impact of changes in the nominal exchange rate on firms that produce export goods. It is not intended to be a comprehensive discussion of international trade issues.

Cantillon effects

Cantillon effects offer a general treatment of the above-discussed problem. Cantillon effects, named after Richard Cantillon, refer to the effect that an excess of money supply has on relative prices in the short run. Cantillon's argument is that newly created money, or newly minted commodity money, enters a particular point, and then spreads through the rest of the market along a particular path. Therefore, prices are affected to a different extent at different points in time and place. In the short run, a nominal shock has non-neutral effects; relative prices are affected. In graphical terms, Cantillon effects means that the demand curves of each particular good at the microlevel shifts at different times, while money neutrality in the short run would imply that *all* demand lines shift at the same time such that all relative prices remain unaffected.

Consider, for instance, a central bank that decides to monetize the deficit of the Treasury. In this case, the government receives newly created money before it has ever been spent. Therefore, the government can increase its purchases *before* prices have increased. As the new money spreads through the market, prices start to increase progressively and unevenly. The last economic agent to receive a share of the newly created money does so *after* prices have increased. This is the reason why inflation is sometimes referred to as a non-legislated tax (the government extracts purchasing power from other economic agents). This is also the reason why under-inflation prices increase unevenly, adding noise, and distortions to relative prices. This is the problem in Lucas's (1972, 1973, 1975) island model.[3]

Since economic agents do not know the exact pattern of how prices are going to be affected, they face a signal extraction problem. Let the price of each good be affected by a positive random shock (ξ), such that the prices observed by the firm are $\hat{p}_i = p_i + \xi_i$ and $\hat{w}_j = w_j + \xi_j$. Then, the value drivers are $\hat{\omega}_i = \dfrac{p_i q_i + q_i \xi}{\hat{p}q}$ and $\hat{\theta}_j = \dfrac{L_j R_j + R_j \xi_j}{\hat{p}q}$.[4] Note the interaction term between a real quantity (q and R) with a nominal shock (ξ). This is the issue captured in the signal extraction problem, a nominal shock (ξ) can be confused with a change in a real variable (q, R). Now Equation 9.4 becomes Equation 9.7.

$$CV_0 = W_0 + \sum_{t=1}^{\infty} f^t \left[\left(\left(\hat{\omega}_{1,t} + \cdots + \hat{\omega}_{n,t} \right) - \left(\hat{\theta}_{1,t} + \cdots + \hat{\theta}_{m,t} \right) \right) \cdot \frac{p_t q_t}{W_{t-1}} - c \right] W_{t-1} \qquad 9.7$$

The value drivers now have a random component (ξ) that produces money illusion. Economic agents observe $\hat{p}$ and $\hat{w}$, but not their components. It is more likely that entrepreneurs would commit mistakes by following noise in a value driver rather than real changes.[5] The more significant the size of the

3 Lucas was also trying to formally capture some of Hayek's insights discussed below.

4 If $\hat{p}_i = p_i + \xi_i$, then $\hat{\omega}_i = \dfrac{(p_i + \xi_i) q_i}{pq} = \dfrac{p_i q_i + q_i \xi_i}{pq}$. Similarly, for $\hat{\omega}$.

5 A few lines above we mentioned how Lucas's islands model also tries to capture this effect. A difference, however, is worth mentioning. In our representation, each price is affected by a *different* random shock. In Lucas's model, all prices are affected by the *same* random shock. If $p_i = z_i + \varepsilon$ represents a real change in a price, then $p_i = z_i + \varepsilon$, where ε is the common random (nominal) shock to all prices. In this sense, Lucas's model does not allow for Cantillon effects since all prices are affected by the same shock at the same time. Differently to our treatment, Lucas's model is emphasizing the signal extraction problem when shocks cannot be perfectly observed.

noise, the more likely entrepreneurs will make these types of mistakes (non-profitable investments).

Consider the following analogy. A pilot (the entrepreneur) is flying a plane but cannot see outside the cockpit window (he does not know what the market equilibrium looks like). However, in the cockpit he has a number of displays (prices, etc.) that provide him with enough information (altitude, speed, direction, etc.) to still successfully fly the plane. If all these measurements were to be biased in the *same* proportion, the information would be inaccurate, but he would still be able to fly the plane to a successful landing. This is the case of nominal shocks without Cantillon effects. However, if these measurements are *randomly* affected, it is very likely that he will make mistakes regardless of how good a pilot he is. This is the case of Cantillon effects.

This Cantillon effects discussion is a second and more general example of how the EVA framework can be molded to capture different effects that explain the behavior of economic agents. A number of other applications and examples can be thought of, but his is enough to make our point on this topic and we can now move on to discuss the next issue.

EVA and the problem of economic calculation under socialism

The socialist-calculation debate at the beginning of the twentieth century was very influential in the development of economic theory. The episode is well known, and we do not need to revisit it at length.[6] However, we can offer a financial translation of some of the arguments put forward in the debate, in particular those of Mises and Hayek.

The start of the debate about the feasibility of socialism was Mises's early work (1920, 1922). Until then, a socialist commonwealth was described as an idealistic society where the question of how to allocate resources was neither asked nor answered. Socialism, at the time, was defined as a regime where there is no private property of the means of production (even if there was private property of *final* consumption goods). In a small society, where there is intimate knowledge among individuals (such as a family), there is no need to allocate resources with a price mechanism. Parents usually do not use a price mechanism to allocate the resources of the household. However, the situation of a large society is different, where there are numerous anonymous interactions, some of which may be repeated and many others of which may not. This anonymity means that individuals do not have knowledge of the

6 For a sample of the literature see Caldwell (1997), Coyne, Leeson, and Boettke (2005), and Hayek (1948).

preference sets of other individuals and also face limited opportunities to learn such preferences. The price mechanism solves the allocation problem *without* information about individuals' preferences.[7]

Mises' challenge consists in raising the question of how resources are to be allocated in a large society. If there is no private property of the means of production, there cannot be market prices for the means of production. If there are no market prices how is their allocation going to be decided? In other words, Mises is asking for an explanation of how the idealistic socialist commonwealth is going to operate rather than for a description of it. Mises's challenge can be interpreted as a critique that socialism is ignoring the *main* question that has to be answered by economics. According to Mises, the effective organization of a large society would not be possible under a socialist regime. Note that, for the sake of argument, Mises assumes away the incentive and public choice problems that would likely exist under a socialist regime with a central planning bureau.

In other words, Mises' argument is not that under socialism prices would be inaccurate or hard to calculate. Rather, he is arguing that the required information would not exist in the first place. Decision-making will be blind. Therefore, the bureau of central planning would have to resort to some other rule to decide how to allocate resources. We can represent Mises' argument in Equation 9.8; because w does not exist $(\nexists)$, therefore CV does not exist either.

$$\underbrace{CV_0}_{\nexists} = W_0 + \sum_{t=1}^{\infty} f^t \cdot \left(\frac{p_t q_t - \overbrace{w_t}^{\nexists} L_t}{W_{t-1}} - c \right) \cdot W_{t-1} \qquad 9.8$$

It is not enough to have prices of final goods (p) and a dollar amount of W_0. As long as w_t does not exist, then CV does not exist either. To be clear, this does not mean that $w_t = 0$, which would result in a *biased* CV, this means that the calculation of CV is not possible.

Hayek (1948, Chapters 2–5) emphasizes the role of *information* and *knowledge* in the problem of resource allocation. While Hayek does not clearly separate these two concepts, he does make use of them (Cachanosky & Padilla, 2017). Information refers to *objective quantitative* data, such as prices, and quantities. This means that information can either be complete or incomplete

7 There are a number of other issues as well. Transactions to be reliable must operate within formal and informal rules and customs. Institutions of law and order are required. The field of institutional economics and the cases of self-governance deal with these types of issues.

(for instance, as in the model of perfect competition). Knowledge is a *subjective* concept. It refers to a state of mind and may be tacit or like knowing how to do things, such as running a business, or explicit such as mathematical knowledge. Hayek spoke of the particular knowledge of a time and place that a local businessperson has but that the bureau of economic analysis cannot possess in statistical form. Because knowledge is a *subjective* concept, it cannot be processed in statistical terms.

For Hayek (and arguably for Mises as well), prices are a *necessary* yet *not a sufficient* condition for markets to achieve equilibrium.[8] The real world is a disequilibrium world, but not a chaotic world. Resources get effectively allocated to productive activities though we cannot know in any objective sense whether any sort of theoretical *maximum* productivity is achieved. *Knowledge* is that qualitative insight that informs economic agents' expectations and allows them to make decisions about *how* resources can be combined. Knowledge is the ability to forecast market prices, and to apply an "EVA" valuation of a firm (what is investment, what are operation costs, how should value drivers be sliced, etc.) This is why Hayek (1948, Chapter 5) refers to competition as a process of discovery (in Hayek 1968 he refers to it as a "discovery" procedure) that requires personal and subjective *knowledge*. An effectively functioning market process needs both information, and knowledge.

We can divide Hayek's argument into three levels to clarify his position. Level one would be that prices are dispersed, and therefore hard to obtain. This level one argument is what socialism advocates purported to deal with using a "trial and error" approach employing numerical methods with a high-power computer. Level two would be that besides dispersed *information*, there is also a *knowledge* problem – how to know which information is the "right" information to have and how to use it. Even if information were to be acquired, there is still the question of how to acquire the right information. Level three is deeper yet. Moving away from the assumptions in level one and two (information exists and is dispersed), level three arguments maintain that the required information *does not exist* outside of the market process. Briefly, if there are no market transactions, then there is no dispersed market information in the first place for the central planner to collect and process. Note that Hayek's level three brings us back to Mises's original critique.

8 A common misreading of Hayek is that he argues that prices are sufficient for market efficiency. See the discussion in Boettke and O'Donnell (2013) See also Lewin (1997b).

Chapter 10

EVA and macroeconomics

We turn now to macroeconomics. This chapter is concerned with the problem of business cycles. Emphasis is given to the Austrian business-cycle theory (ABCT). There are a few reasons for this.

First, the ABCT fits nicely into a financial framework.[1] We show that a macroeconomic implication of our approach can be interpreted as a financial foundation of the ABCT. Furthermore, the problems surrounding the *average period of production* are a significant source of the weakness associated with the ABCT. As discussed at length in this book, the APP can be interpreted as the Macaulay duration of a cash flow. In contrast to the APP, duration is a widely used and a well-understood financial construct. Therefore, the distinctive characteristic and foundation of the ABCT (the effect of interest-rate movements on APP) is on more solid ground considered from a financial point of view.

A second reason is the renewed interest shown in this business-cycle theory in the last decade. The 2008 financial crisis provided a major challenge to a number of mainstream business-cycle theories and, directly, or indirectly, a number of explanations turned to the distinctive insights of the ABCT and those of the "Austrian school of economics" to explain what went wrong in 2008 (Borio & Disyatat, 2011; Caballero, 2010; Cachanosky & Salter, 2017; Calvo, 2013; Diamond & Rajan, 2009, 2012; Hume & Sentance, 2009; Leijonhufvud, 2009). Given the financial nature of the 2008 crisis, and the renewed interest in the ABCT, a focus on the financial foundations of this theory can provide a pathway to novel business-cycle research.

The Austrian business-cycle theory (ABCT): a credit-induced business cycle

A challenge faced by the ABCT is that different authors may emphasize different characteristics of this theory, or even arrive at similar conclusions

1 See also Cachanosky (2015a), Cachanosky and Lewin (2016b), and Lewin and Cachanosky (2016).

through different lines of reasoning. Mises's (1949, Chapter XX) explanation is not the same, for instance, as that of Hayek (1931). One of the best well-known contemporary expositions of the ABCT is Garrison's model (2001). Garrison's work, however, is designed as a pedagogical tool for economics education and, as such, emphasizes some particular characteristics while ignoring others. These differences represent variations on a common theme; there is a common thread of argument across all the different expositions of this theory.

The economic intuition behind the ABCT is quite straightforward. An "Austrian" business cycle is a credit-induced boom-bust sequence that results from investors, entrepreneurs or both reacting to a cost of capital (the interest rate) that is too low to be sustained, such as when the central bank reduces short-term interest rates below their market rate (the rates that would spontaneously clear the market for loanable funds). When, sooner, or later, the monetary authority faces the need to increase the interest rate, investors will then face a situation where some past investments will be shown to be unprofitable, particularly those investments whose value and profitability are relatively more sensitive to movements in the cost of capital (the discount rate). We know that this means that investments with higher duration (D) will be affected the most since D measures both the amount of time involved in any investment and the interest-rate sensitivity of the project's value. In effect, investors will have to reduce the "allocation of time" to their production process. This is, in a nutshell, what constitutes a boom-and-bust business cycle in the ABCT and captures the central idea in all of the different ways in which this theory may be represented.

The low interest rate triggers both an increase in consumption, and an increase in investment. This is the tension usually highlighted in a typical ABCT exposition. Eventually, economic agents realize that there are not enough resources for both uses and something has to give, triggering the bust.

The ABCT was originally developed in the early twentieth century. It is important to contextualize two aspects of that period. The first is that, at the time the ABCT was being originally developed, the industrial sector was a more significant part of the GDP than it is today. This explains a particular concern with how movements in interest rates affect (physical) capital intensity (for an example see the treatment in Robbins, 1934). As we have shown in previous chapters, the key variable, however, is time (or duration), not capital intensity. The second is the presence of the gold standard as the monetary regime in place. In such a monetary regime, if a central bank over-expands the circulation of its convertible banknotes it starts to lose reserves as a consequence. Therefore, eventually the central bank will have to revise its monetary policy, increasing the interest rate, and triggering an ABCT-type business cycle. This was a major problem at the time of World War I and was also one of the reasons why the ABCT is associated with the Great Depression.[2] In the case of fiat currencies, the trigger point that reverses an expansionary monetary policy is, as it were, more psychological, it is the level of inflation that the monetary authority considers unacceptable.[3]

It is also important to note that the ABCT is not just a theory of business cycles based on an excess of money supply. It is, more specifically, a *credit*-induced business-cycle theory. When a central bank enters into an expansionary policy, the newly printed money is spent *first* by the Treasury (a government-spending shock) and this triggers a number of imbalances sooner or later to be corrected, but this would not be an ABCT story. The ABCT requires that the injection point of the monetary expansion be the *credit* market. An excess of credit would induce a fall in the interest rate *before* other prices rise (due to inflation). This represents a particular change in the relative price of time with respect to intermediate and final goods, which is what drives the particular dynamics of the ABCT and is also the point of interest of the next section. It is, in short, what allows for a financial interpretation of the ABCT that fits with the discussion of the previous chapters.

The ABCT does not imply that any credit expansion would trigger an ABCT type of crisis. Consider that central banks that target an interest rate usually choose a short-term rate (money market), such as the federal funds rate. Yet, investment projects are evaluated with long-term interest rates. Therefore, for a credit expansion to put into motion an ABCT cycle, the expansionary policy has to have an effect on the discount rate used by investors to calculate the present value of different investment projects. Of course, this may, or may not happen.

The ABCT, like any theory, allows for different levels of generality depending on which conditional assumptions are used. The exposition in this section is quite general. The more specific a theory becomes, the more conditional assumptions need to be included in the theory. This means that it is possible that a theory appears to fail empirically not because of logical inconsistencies, but because one, or more of the conditional assumptions do not hold. It is not the theory itself, but its *application*, that is problematic. For instance, a contemporary exposition of the ABCT may need to assume a

2 A detailed discussion of the Great Depression, the ABCT, and the gold standard far exceeds the purpose of this book and this chapter. Our limited purpose is to call attention to the historical context and some of the reasons why the ABCT is associated with the Great Depression.

3 Another issue raised by analyzing a fiat money situation (rather than assuming an international gold standard) is the role of exchange rates. What are, for instance, the dynamics of the crisis if there are flexible or fixed exchange rates? See Cachanosky (2014a, 2014b, 2015b), Cachanosky and Hoffmann (2016), Hoffmann (2010), and Hoffmann and Cachanosky (2018)

fiat currencies context with exchange rates rather than an international gold standard. In addition, specific regulatory assumptions are needed to explain why a crisis such as the 2008 subprime crisis took place in the housing market and not in another particular industry.[4]

Finally, the ABCT does not claim to be the *only* valid business-cycle theory. The ABCT should be seen as a theory that explains why a credit-induced boom may be unsustainable, but not as a theory that can explain the particularities of the bust. It is possible, and most likely also necessary, to combine the ABCT with other theories and facts to explain big economic events. For instance, to explain the Great Depression one can resort to the ABCT (plus historically specific conditional assumptions) to explain the 1920s, and to Fisher's (1933) debt-deflation theory and Friedman and Schwartz (1963) money supply contraction to explain the crash of 1929. Also, Higgs's (2009) regime uncertainty in addition to market regulations can be used to explain why the crisis lasted so long.[5]

Financial foundations of the ABCT

According to the ABCT, a reduction of the discount rate (c) below its free market or natural level results in investing in relatively long-term projects. We need, then, to link movements in the discount rate to changes in relative prices that would incentivize more investment in projects with higher duration.

This is now easy to show. We know that the capital-value of a project (CV) is the present value of its expected cash flow. We also know that the project's cash flow has a duration (D) that depends on the life and pattern of the cash flow. In addition, we know that modified duration is also a measure of CV sensitivity to changes in c.

It follows, then, that when c falls, the CV of all projects rise, but they do so at different rates. Those cash flows with a higher D will see their CVs increase more than those projects with a lower D. This produces two effects. The first one is a change in the relative CV of each project. The second one is a potential change in the *ranking* of the project according to their CVs. Consider an investor who has a portfolio of potential projects to invest in. These projects are ranked by their CVs (or, similarly, by their $NPVs$). If the discount rate

4 On the role of conditional assumptions and empirical verification in economics see the still informative discussion by Machlup (1955). For a more contemporary discussion see Caldwell (1984) and Zanotti and Cachanosky (2015).

5 This is particularly true of booms initiated by waves of innovation, but sustained beyond their natural life by expansionary monetary policy (like the dot.com boom–bust of the late 1990s to March 2001). It is an Austrian story containing important Schumpeterian and political business-cycle insights.

falls, then all *CVs* increase, but their ranking may also change. This means that, at the margin, the allocation of resources will be shifted from lower to higher *D* projects. The larger the interest-rate deviation from its equilibrium level and the longer the low interest-rate policy is in effect the more resources will be misallocated and the larger the business cycle will look. When the monetary authority decides to reverse its policy and increase the interest rate, the opposite effects happen. The *CVs* of all projects fall, but those projects with a higher *D* see their *CVs* fall even faster than projects with a lower *D*. Now the relative price signal calls for reallocations of resources from longer to shorter projects. The low interest rate makes all projects look more profitable (the same investment returns a higher *CV*). When the interest rate goes back to its equilibrium level, investors find either that their projects are less profitable than expected, or that they are actually not sustainable at the now higher discount rate. The former project may still survive in the market, but the latter ones will have to be liquidated or face bankruptcy.

The following simulation illustrates these effects. Consider five projects that require the same initial investment. The first one produces a free-cash flow of $100 for 20 periods. The second one produces a free-cash flow of $175 for ten periods. The third one produces a free-cash flow of $325 for five periods. The fourth one produces a free-cash flow of $115 in the first period increasing at a ten-percent rate for ten periods. The fifth and final one produces a free-cash flow of $400 in the first period decreasing at a rate of 20 percent for ten periods. This scenario has a total of five cash flows, the first three ones are regular cash flows, and the two last ones are irregular cash flows. Now assume that in period one the discount rate is five percent, in period two the discount rate is four percent, and so on until period five where the discount rate is one percent. Figure 10.1 shows how the *CV* of each project changes for each different discount rate (see the appendix for the table with the numbers used in the plot).

This scenario highlights some features. Consider first that, as expected, all CVs increase as the discount rate falls, but they do so to different degrees. For instance, CV1 is the one that increases most because it is the project with the higher duration (see appendix for complete data). CV3 is the one that increases at a slower rate because this is the one with the lowest duration. Second, compare CV4, and 5. CV5 has a higher weight of cash flows in near periods, while CV4 has a higher weight of cash flows in future periods. These two cash flows are constructed to highlight how these two different patterns are differently affected by changes in the discount rate. If CV4 represents "long-term" projects and CV5 represents economic activities closer to final consumption, then the former is affected to a larger extent than the latter. Note that even

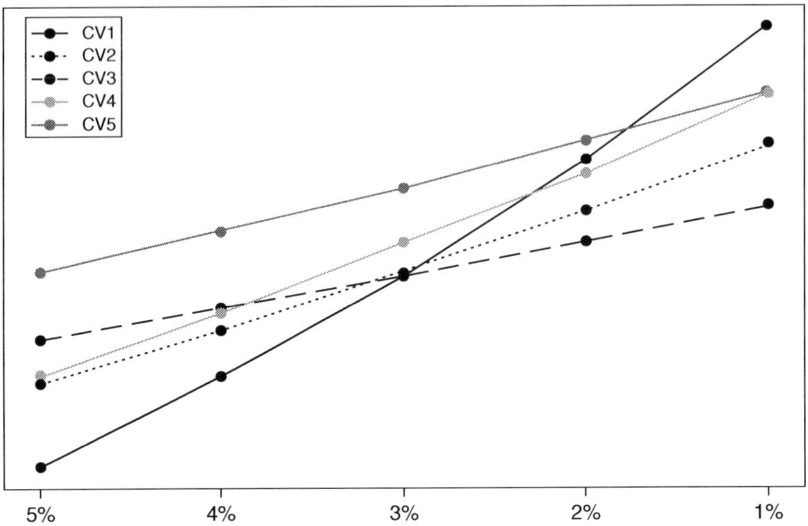

Figure 10.1 Present values (vertical axis) at different discount rates (horizontal axis).

Notes
CV1 = Present value of $100 for 20 periods.
CV2 = Present value of $175 for ten periods.
CV3 = Present value of $325 for five periods.
CV4 = Present value of $115 increasing at a 10-percent rate for ten periods.
CV5 = Present value of $400 decreasing at a 20-percent rate for 20 periods.

if these two projects have the same number of periods their durations are different. Finally, because each project sees its CV change to a different degree (because they have different durations), the ranking of projects can change significantly. At a discount rate of five percent, CV1 ranks last, but at a discount rate of one percent CV1 climbs to the top. Alternatively, the project that ranks first at a discount rate of five percent falls to third position when the discount rate is one percent.

Another way to phrase this last effect is by ranking the projects in terms of their duration. Let us assume that we have three projects, one with high duration (HD), one with medium duration (MD), and one with low duration (LD). Then we know that all relative prices in terms of higher with respect to lower duration will increase. Namely, all three $\frac{CV_{HD}}{CV_{MD}}, \frac{CV_{HD}}{CV_{LD}}$, and $\frac{CV_{MD}}{CV_{LD}}$ will increase (decrease) when the discount rate falls (rises). This is the financial microfoundation of the ABCT. This representation captures the required

Table 10.1 Rankings at different discount rates

	Period 1 5%	*Period 2* 4%	*Period 3* 3%	*Period 4* 2%	*Period 5* 1%
CV1	5	5	5	2	1
CV2	4	4	3	4	4
CV3	2	2	4	5	5
CV4	3	3	2	3	2
CV5	1	1	1	1	3

relative price change for the ABCT story to be grounded in consistent economic reasoning.[6]

Consider now the following implications of the financial framework of the ABCT. The first one is that this financial treatment makes it clearer that the ABCT *does not* depend on any type of Cantillon effects (discussed in the previous chapter). The Austrian literature may be right in emphasizing the Cantillon effects of an expansionary monetary policy. However, such emphasis is usually framed in terms of the relative price of final (and maybe intermediate) goods. However, all that the ABCT needs is the discount rate (the price of time) to fall with respect to cash flows. A "pure" ABCT effect can be constructed by assuming money neutrality in the short run and letting the discount rate fall. Consider formula 10.8. All that needs to happen is that f^t increases; the ABCT story does not need a Cantillon effect that would have an effect on EVA or its value drivers. Furthermore, the theory would be inconsistent if it claimed to explain business cycles with changes in the interest rate but could not do so without assuming changes in *other* relative prices.

$$CV = W_0 + \sum_{t=1}^{\infty} f^t \left(\frac{\sum_{i=1}^{n} p_{i,t} q_{i,t} - \sum_{j=1}^{m} w_{j,t} L_{j,t}}{W_{t-1}} - c \right) W_{t-1} \qquad 10.1$$

To be sure, the change in relative CVs may be considered a type of Cantillon effect. If so, what we argue is that the ABCT rests on this *specific* case of Cantillon effect and *does not need* other ones. In fact, this is the scenario we

6 In a previous study we find, for a selected number of firms, that a fall in the discount rate is correlated with an increase in the profits perceived by firms and firm size (net investment) consistent with the expected result (Cachanosky & Lewin, 2016a).

show above in Equation 10.1. Second, we do not claim that money is neutral in the short run, what we show is that the ABCT is robust to this assumption. Even though the ABCT enjoys only a marginal presence in the mainstream treatment of business cycles, the above arguments show that this theory is not that far away from already existing formal treatments. There are two problems that need to be tied together. The first one is the problem of optimal duration, where the duration of a chosen production process can be affected by monetary policy (Hendrickson & Salter, 2016). The second one is the issue of irreversible investments (Dixit & Pyndick, 1994).[7] In other words, once the misunderstandings surrounding the problem of the average period of production are resolved (with the use of duration), then the ABCT looks like a much more appealing business-cycle theory from a formal mainstream point of view.

Rational expectations and the ABCT

Even though a financial framing of the ABCT brings clarity and consistency to the theory, other objections still require discussion. Although a financial approach allows us to ground the ABCT in relative price changes (financial microfoundations), the theory remains open to a rational-expectations type of critique (Caplan, 1997, Cowen, 1997, p. 77, Tullock, 1988, 1989). To wit, the critique maintains that the ABCT does not explain why all entrepreneurs make the same mistake of investing in projects that are *too long* when monetary policy is known and why the same entrepreneurs make the same mistake more than once when the monetary authority repeatedly lowers the interest rate.

A case can be made regarding to what extent the assumption of rational expectations is applicable (see Caballero, 2010). Expectations do have a *subjective* component. This does not mean that expectations are irrational. Expectations are, using Garrison's (1986) term, *a*rational.[8] Our intention here is not to question the use and misuse of rational expectations, but rather to use this critique to shed more light on the ABCT dynamics.

Certainly, the problem of expectations is hardly new with respect to the ABCT. Lachmann (1940) argues that as long as entrepreneurs adjust their expectations to the known effects of monetary policy, an ABCT type of business cycle would not be possible. Entrepreneurs will not be fooled by an interest rate that is unsustainably low and will use realistic discount rates that motivate them to avoid projects that are *too long*. Mises (1943) reply is interesting, he acknowledges that to the extent that entrepreneurs "learn"

7 For an example of recent formal treatment of ABCT topics see and Hendrickson and Salter (2016) and Hendrickson (2017).

8 See also the discussion in Eusepi and Preson (2011) and Fuster and Mendel (2010).

about the ABCT, this type of cycle will become less severe and frequent. However, there is no guarantee that such learning will take place.

There are a few reasons why entrepreneurs may fail to learn from the historical experience of cycles. The first one is that the market is not populated by representative entrepreneurs; the market is populated by a large population of disparate entrepreneurs. These entrepreneurs not only have different worldviews, they also go through generational changes. This means that the next generation of entrepreneurs may forget what the previous generation had learned. The second reason is that each generation of entrepreneurs may learn different lessons from the *same* data. Why would this be the case? Because even though data is *objective*, data processing (understanding) is *subjective*. The ABCT, right, or wrong, is only one of a large number of business cycle theories. The same data can be consistent with more than one theory at the same time (the prediction of two theories may be the same but for different reasons). A third reason is that things become more complicated when we realize that the same monetary policy that would trigger a business cycle according to the ABCT can take place under different regulatory frameworks, policies, etc. The dynamics of the business cycle, then, would look different. In the real world the *ceteris paribus* does not hold, making data interpretation more challenging. Since data interpretation and expectations are subjective, there is no reason to assume that the "average" lesson from a business cycle experience must be the right one.

The Austrian literature has dealt with the rational expectations critique in different ways. Challenging the representative entrepreneur assumption, Callahan and Horwitz (2010) argue for two types of entrepreneurs, the *savvy, and* the *naïve*. The former knows that the low interest rate is out of equilibrium, but the latter does not. In this framework, the ABCT is driven by the *naïve* entrepreneur. With a similar argument, Evans and Baxendale (2008) focus on the role of the *marginal* entrepreneur: the one individual who is willing to invest in long-term projects when the interest rate is below its equilibrium value. Another approach is that of Carilli and Dempster (2001), who argue that the boom is rational. In this argument, entrepreneurs know that the interest rate is out of equilibrium and the economy is on an unsustainable path, yet, the rational behavior is to invest in the *too long* projects and sell their projects before the crash.[9]

The financial framework of the ABCT adds another layer to the analysis mentioned in the previous paragraph. Instead of assuming only two types of entrepreneurs (*savvy* and *naïve*), assume a continuum of entrepreneurs with

9 Instead of adopting the rational-expectations critique, other authors criticize the rational-expectations assumption in the first place (Barnett & Block, 2005, 2006; Block, 2001; O'Driscoll & Rizzo, 1985, pp. 213–226).

different expectations about the natural or equilibrium rate of interest (i_N). Further, assume a normal distribution around i_N such that errors are not biased: $E[i] = i_N$.

Assume now that the central bank reduces the interest rate to some level below i_N. Then we know that, even if expectations are correct "on average," some entrepreneurs do think that the actual lowered interest-rate level is the correct one. The financial framework we have developed suggests the consequences of this. We know that if the interest rate falls, the present value of all projects increases, but it does so to different degrees. Projects with higher D are more sensitive to reductions in the discount rate. Therefore, those entrepreneurs who consider the low interest rate to be the correct one, are *willing*, and *able* to finance projects with higher duration. Since high duration projects see their values increase at a higher rate than lower duration projects (and their ranking among competing projects may change as well), these entrepreneurs are able to outbid entrepreneurs in the market for factors of production who rationally discount projects at a higher interest rate.

As discussed above, the longer, and the farther the interest rate is out of equilibrium, the larger the amount of unprofitable investment is likely to be accumulated. When, sooner, or later, the interest-rate returns to its sustainable level, these investments prove to have a lower rate of return than expected or be unprofitable. The key point, to put it simply, is that even though *expectational errors* around the mean may "cancel out" ($E[i] = i_N$), the *effect* of the errors do not (the present values of different projects have *different* elasticities with respect to i).

The rational-expectations critique has triggered different reactions. Some of the defenses have been mentioned above. Others recommend reconstructing the ABCT. Cowen (1997) recommends rebuilding the ABCT to focus on risk rather than period of production. Young (2015) offers an attempt to work along these lines. Wagner (1999) recommends building an agent framework with divergent (heterogeneous) rather than convergent (homogeneous) expectations. In a similar line, Salter and Luther (2016, p. 52) recommend discarding the period of production and focusing on any type of resource misallocation.

Certainly, the above-mentioned lines of research can have value on their own, and we do not dispute that important insights are to be learned from these research projects. We merely suggest here that the ABCT can be consistently framed in financial terms. By consistently, we point to two features. First, that the theory has (financial) microfoundations, meaning the cycle can be explained in terms of relative price changes. Secondly, the theory is robust to rational expectations as long as one is willing to accept that the real world is populated by different entrepreneurs with expectations based on different "models" of the world.

Extensions of the ABCT

Exchange rates

This financial application of the ABCT also allows for extensions or adding and modifying assumptions of the model. One case is the role of exchange rates in business cycle dynamics. We do not need to repeat the discussion and formulas used in the previous chapter. It is enough to add some historical context and potential implications.

While the canonical version of the ABCT may still prove to be useful as a general approach to monetary policy effects, the theory also needs to be updated to contemporary monetary regimes to offer a better explanation of business-cycle dynamics and be a good fit to present market conditions.[10]

Recall that the ABCT was developed within the context of a gold standard regime. Under this monetary arrangement, all countries share the same currency: gold. Therefore, there was no particular need to deal with exchange rates (the price of two *different* currencies). Today we have a very different monetary setting, each central bank issues its own fiat money as an ultimate means of payment, whereas under the gold standard each central bank issues a banknote redeemable (i.e., convertible) into gold (the ultimate means of payment). The difference is important, since under fiat currencies, exchange rates play a crucial role. Since there is more than one ultimate means of payment, their relative prices can also affect how resources are allocated.

In the typical ABCT story, the interest rate is the only channel of transmission of resource misallocation. The relative price of time is reduced, and therefore more "duration is consumed." With fiat currencies, the ABCT has two channels of transmission affecting resource misallocation. The interest rate for duration, and the exchange rate for tradable and non-tradable goods.

This opens questions for research such as how do the ABCT dynamics change under different exchange-rate regimes. For instance, it is possible that a floating exchange-rate regime would shield a small open economy (the periphery) from an ABCT type of business cycle driven by a major central bank (the center)?

The exchange-rate effects can be captured by modifying the capital-value formula by adding the exchange rate to it and tracking changes in relative present values when interest rates move. The capital-value of a project will be impacted by two variables: the interest rate and the exchange rate. The effect of the latter will depend on where the exchange rate is added to the calculation and on the exchange-rate regime in place. In other words, the canonical ABCT has one channel through which monetary policy produces market distortions. The exchange rate is a second channel.

10 For some research advancing this line of inquiry, see Cachanosky (2014b, 2014a, 2015b), Hoffmann (2010) and Hoffmann and Schnabl (2011).

Risk

Another possible extension is adding risk into the ABCT financial framework, as suggested by Cowen (1997) and Young (2015). This is a straightforward addition in the form of a risk premium (σ) to the discount rate. Let i_N be the natural rate of interest, then $c^* = i_N + \sigma$, where c^* is the risk-adjusted rate of equilibrium. For instance, different industries may have a different i^* even if they have the same i_N, the reason being that these industries face a different risk premium.

Consider now Equation 10.2, which shows the capital-value calculation including the risk premium in the discount rate.

$$CV_0 = K_0 + \sum_{t=1}^{T} \frac{\left(ROIC - (i_N + \sigma)\right) K_{t-1}}{\left(1 + i_N + \sigma\right)^t} \qquad 10.2$$

Consider, for the sake of argument, a policy that reduces the risk associated to an asset with a long cash flow of services, such as a house. The reduction in risk premium may not be because market conditions are improving and risk falls, but because the government (implicitly or explicitly) guarantees a bailout to mortgages should financial distress happen. The effect, then, would be similar to policy that reduces the interest rate in that particular market. Or consider, alternatively, a policy that reduces the interest rate to all sectors, yet there is a second policy that specifically reduces risk in one industry. This would produce a bias in how CVs react to the *pure* interest-rate effect. Now it is possible that the change in CV rankings is different from what it would be if c (i in the equation) were the only variable being modified.

Risk is an important variable to consider, especially in the context of recent business cycles. A financial framework allows for an easy way to include this variable into the analysis. Different historical applications may require more emphasis on discount rate manipulations, other historical applications may require more emphasis in risk premium changes. Either approach is feasible and, also, in the way we presented it above, it can be seen to have similar effects. This is, of course, because σ is one of the components included in the discount rate c.

Appendix

Table 10.2 Present value and duration value of projects included in Figure 10.1.

	Period 1 5%		*Period 2* 4%		*Period 3* 3%		*Period 4* 2%		*Period 5* 1%	
	Present value	*Duration*	*Present value*	*Duration*	*Present value*	*Duration*	*Present value*	*Duration*	*Present value*	*Duration*
CV1	$1,246.20	8.9	$1,359.00	9.21	$1,487.70	9.52	$1,653.10	9.84	$1,804.60	10.17
CV2	$1,351.30	5.1	$1,419.40	5.18	$1,492.80	5.26	$1,572.00	5.34	$1,657.50	5.42
CV3	$1,407.10	2.9	$1,446.80	2.92	$1,488.40	2.94	$1,531.90	2.96	$1,577.40	2.98
CV4	$1,362.40	5.88	$1,441.80	5.96	$1,527.80	6.04	$1,621.20	6.12	$1,722.50	6.2
CV5	$1,494.50	3.49	$1,545.80	3.55	$1,600.20	3.61	$1,658.00	3.67	$1,719.60	3.73

CV1 = Present value of $100 for 20 periods.
CV2 = Present value of $175 for ten periods.
CV3 = Present value of $325 for five periods.
CV4 = Present value of $115 increasing at a 10-percent rate for ten periods.
CV5 = Present value of $400 decreasing at a 20-percent rate for 20 periods.

Chapter 11

EVA and institutions

This book has been concerned with both microeconomic and macroeconomic issues. In particular, it has dealt with problems related to capital theory such as the period of production and the value of capital, as well as business cycles. This chapter offers a general application to institutional issues. Behavior at the microeconomic level produces macroeconomic results. And, in turn, microeconomic behavior depends on the set of incentives determined by the institutional framework in which economic agents are immersed.

First, we offer a general discussion of institutions to frame our discussion. We then comment on EVA and macroeconomic performance. Finally, we map different dimensions of economic freedom into an EVA analysis. A vast literature from Adam Smith until today shows that market-friendly institutions lead to higher levels of income.[1] We show how to map economic freedom into an EVA framework.

Why are institutions important?

It is typical to define institutions as the formal (such as laws, regulations, etc.) and informal (such as culture, customs, etc.) rules of behavior in a society. In other words, the "rules of the game." It is also common to use sports analogies. The way basketball players approach the game depends on the rules of game. For instance, we can predict that changing the points awarded for long-distance baskets from three to four would result in more long-distance shots. By changing the rules of basketball, we can make the game look completely different. Institutional changes can result in major changes in the behavior of economic agents.

1 The literature on institutions is immense. For a sample see Acemoglu and Robinson (2012), (1975; 1985), Coyne (2008), Dixit (2009), Easterly (Easterly, 2008), Gwartney, Holcombe, and Lawson (2004), Hayek (1973, 1976, 1979), North (1991), Olson (2000), Ostrom (2010), and Williamson (2009).

Institutions play an important role in establishing the incentives that economic agents face. In terms of categories developed by Acemoglu and Robinson (2012), institutions can be *extractive*, or *inclusive*. The former is an institutional framework that facilitates rent extraction by politicians and interest groups. The latter is an institutional framework that promotes economic efficiency. The former results in underdeveloped and poor economies. The latter results in developed and wealthy economies. A salient example is the contrast between North Korea and South Korea. These two countries share a similar history, culture, language, geography, natural resources, etc. The main difference between the two Koreas is the institutional framework that governs each country (Korea was divided into North and South after World War II). There are numerous other examples.

The relationship between institutions and economic performance thus rests on the relationship between incentives and economic performance. Institutions are important because, in the long run, the level of income (and wealth) depends on the incentives established by the institutional framework. While economic policy can affect short-term business outcomes around a trend, the institutional framework more fundamentally affects the long-run income level (high or low) around which business cycles occur. This is the reason why, for an economy to evolve from an underdeveloped (low-income) to a developed (high-income) economy, policy is not enough – institutional reforms are needed.[2] The more market-friendly (inclusive) institutions there are, the higher the level of income and general wellbeing will be.

EVA and macroeconomic performance

It should be obvious that EVA outcomes are not independent of the institutional framework in which economic agents are immersed. A well-functioning healthy economy will reveal higher and more stable levels of EVA. Firms capture profits in a macroeconomic environment that is more or less stable. Positive values of EVA at the macroeconomic level imply economic growth.

Broadly speaking, a firm can achieve high levels of EVA in three ways. First, by securing a high rate of revenue earned on capital invested. Second, by having low production costs. Third, by having a low discount rate (opportunity cost of invested capital). These three variables can be affected by both institutions and economic policy. For instance, high taxes will result in low rates of return by affecting revenues, costs or both; an insecure environment for property rights will result in a higher discount rate after adjusting for risk.

2 Consider cases such as that of Chile, China, India, or Ireland.

Perhaps most important, institutions define the limits within which entrepreneurial creativity and alertness operates. The reason why countries with extractive institutions do not have successful entrepreneurs is not the lack of entrepreneurial creativity, it is because of the strict limits imposed by the institutions of these countries. For instance, the same entrepreneur, successful in the United States, could not be so in a country such as the Soviet Union or communist Cuba. Inefficient institutions can have the undesired effect of diverting entrepreneurial creativity and energy away from market and product development into navigating complicated regulatory requirements, satisfying arbitrary standards from regulatory agencies, or engaging in rent-seeking activities.[3] In the next section we discuss in more detail how different institutions and policies affect EVA results and therefore economic efficiency.

Mapping economic freedom into an EVA analysis

To frame our discussion, we use the Economic Freedom of the World (EFW) index published by the Fraser Institute. While there are a number of indices available, there are two reasons why the EFW is convenient for our purpose here. The first one is that it acts as a proxy for economic freedom, in that there is a correlation between market-friendly institutions and the levels of income mentioned above. The second one is that it also provides a wide range of different measures from monetary policy, to taxes, to international trade, to property rights security. In addition, the EFW is widely used in academic research (Hall & Lawson, 2014).

The EFW is divided into five areas: (1) size of government, (2) legal system and property rights, (3) sound money, (4) freedom to trade internationally, and (5) regulation. The rationale for including size of government is that the larger the participation of the state in total spending, the more decision-making by households and firms is crowded out. The legal system and property rights relate to how well laws protect justly the acquired property of economic agents. Sound money focuses on inflation rates and price volatility. High inflation rates work as taxes that extract value from economic agents and inflation volatility makes it difficult to accurately make business plan forecasts. Freedom to trade internationally refers to trade openness. Regulation, generally, refers to regulation that restricts domestic trade.[4]

We can now proceed to map the five areas of the EFW into the EVA framework. This allows us to be more specific on how different institutions affect

3 For a classic treatment see Baumol (1990). Also see Padilla and Cachanosky (2016).

4 For a more detailed discussion see Gwartney, Lawson, Hall, and Murphy (2018).

economic activity and the relative impact that each area has. We first proceed to map shocks to EFW sub-indices into an EVA framework, then we proceed to offer a general presentation of how EVA outcomes can be affected in different ways (through revenue, costs, and discount rates).

EFW area 1: size of government

The larger the government, in terms of spending, the more resources the state must extract from the private sector either in the form of taxes or government debt. Consider first the case of taxes on revenue. Let τ be the tax rate and the other variables as defined in the previous chapters. Equation 11.1 captures the tax effect.

$$CV = W_0 + \sum_{t=1}^{\infty} \frac{1}{(1+c)^t} \left(\frac{\sum_{i=1}^{n} (p_{i,t} q_{i,t})(1-\tau) - \sum_{j=1}^{m} w_{j,t} L_{j,t}}{W_{t-1}} - c \right) W_{t-1} \quad 11.1$$

Compare this equation with the case of government spending financed with sovereign debt instead of taxes. In this case the increased demand for loanable funds produces a higher interest rate. Let c_g be the effect of sovereign debt on the market discount rate as shown in Equation 11.2.[5] The value of c_g depends on the amounts loaned by the government as well as the elasticity of the supply of loanable funds.

$$CV = W_0 + \sum_{t=1}^{\infty} \frac{1}{(1+c+c_g)^t} \left(ROIC_t - (c+c_g) \right) W_{t-1} \quad 11.2$$

Compare the two equations. In the case of taxes, the negative impact on CV occurs because of a reduction in the NOPAT of the firm. In the second case, c_g has two effects. First, as a reduction in EVA $\left(ROIC - (c + c_G) \right)$, in each time period. Second, as a higher discount rate $\left(1 + c + c_g\right)$. Note that this second effect takes place in a term that grows at an exponential rate. It follows that if government debt has an impact on the discount rate, then its effect on EVA can be larger than that of direct taxation. Certainly, the impact on the discount rate may be smaller than τ on the EVA of each period, but

5 We are assuming the increase in the interest rate increases the discount rate used by decision-makers.

the exponential growth of the discount factor can amount to a significant accumulated effect, especially for long-term projects.

EFW area 2: legal system and property rights

The lack of legal protection of property rights translates into a risk of expropriation and confiscation. This type of risk is captured as a country risk premium in the discount rate (φ). The higher the risk of expropriation, the higher the rate of return that will be required by investors; therefore a country risk premium is added to the risk-free discount rate just as is common practice in financial valuation.

$$CV = W_0 + \sum_{t=1}^{\infty} \frac{1}{(1+c+\varphi)^t} \left(\frac{\sum_{i=1}^{n} (p_{i,t} q_{i,t}) - \sum_{j=1}^{m} w_{j,t} L_{j,t}}{W_{t-1}} - (c+\varphi) \right) W_{t-1} \qquad 11.3$$

Note that country risk affects CV in two ways, similar to the case of an increase in government debt to finance higher levels of spending. One, through a lower EVA in each period (a lower $p_{i,t}q_{i,t}$). Two, through a larger discount rate in a term that grows at an exponential rate. There are a number of problems and economic issues that arise when property rights are not well defined or protected. However, what we are most interested in showing is that economies with an unsafe property-rights environment (a high value of φ) tend to have lower rates of returns and economic activities with lower durations. As mentioned above, a poor institutional framework sets a constraint on how much profit residents in an economy can be expected to earn. The reason is that the discount rate, which includes the risk premium, increases at an exponential rate and economic returns are usually subject to decreasing marginal returns. These means that a number of economic activities that require long maturation terms (durations) will not be profitable options regardless of how savvy and creative entrepreneurs are.

An institutional reform that reduces the discount rate can have a significant impact on CVs across the whole economy. Expected economic profits increase *and* get discounted at a lower discount rate. Since longer cash flows are affected to a larger extent, it is to be expected that the new situation will imply economic activities operating at higher duration values. This is the financial equivalent of Adam Smith's size of the market or Menger's lengthening of production activities as the market grows. As an illustration, consider the case of free market reforms in countries such as China, India, or Ireland. These market-friendly reforms increased the rate of return across the board, but at a higher rate in projects with higher duration.

EFW area 3: sound money

In a previous chapter we discussed how to capture Cantillon effects produced by inflation in the EVA framework. The focus of that exercise is to highlight the short-run non-neutral effects on relative prices and therefore that, at least to some extent, resources will be misallocated. Here we want to emphasize another problem, namely, how the standard deviation of the inflation rate affects the range of the CV of any project. For an investor making plans in a high inflation environment, the range of potential economic results is broader than in an economy with low inflation rates. In other words, the confidence interval of CV broadens, the larger the standard deviation on inflation. Therefore, it is more likely that any given project will actually face losses rather than profits. The result is an increase in entrepreneurial mistakes, that is, an increase in economic activities that either yield lower rates of return or losses instead of the expected profits. To be sure over a certain range the likelihood of profits (the expected CV or EVA) also rises as a result of greater overall variance. The increase in the variance of returns is something that will favor "gamblers" who are less risk averse and will discourage investments for those with more "normal" levels of risk aversion. This is shown in Figure 11.1 discussed below.

Consider this effect in Equation 11.4, where $\sigma_{(\mathrm{EVA})}$ captures the standard deviation of EVA due to inflation. The feature we want to highlight is that higher inflation rates produce higher values of $\sigma_{(\mathrm{EVA})}$.

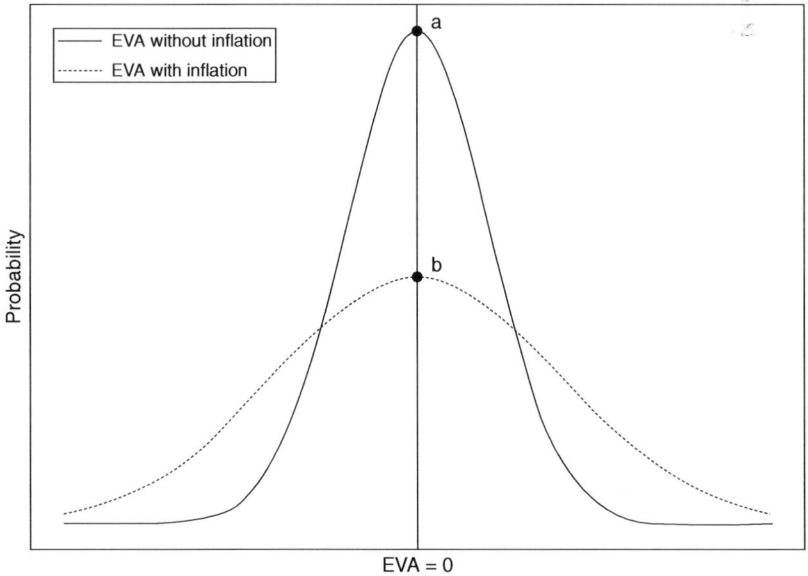

Figure 11.1 Effect of inflation on EVA likelihood.

$$CV = W_0 + \sum_{t=1}^{\infty} \frac{1}{(1+c)^t} (EVA_t \pm \sigma_{(EVA)}) \quad 11.4$$

As EVA values take a wider range, then the probability of observing “false profits” increases (Figure 11.1). The solid line represents the situation without inflation. Let us assume an economy in equilibrium such that firms receive normal returns whereby economic profits, or EVA, equals zero. The dotted line represents the case of inflation, where $\sigma_{(EVA)}$ is now higher. The distance $a-b$ represents the expected probability gap of a given result. In short, economic activities become riskier. *Ceteris paribus*, this effect decreases the likelihood of normal returns and increases the likelihood of large profits and large losses.

EFW area 4: freedom to trade internationally

We have also seen a simple adaptation to international trade in Chapter 9, where the focus was on the role played by the exchange rate. The analysis of a trade restriction such as tariffs to either export or import follows naturally from that exposition. The effect of a tariff (either on imports or exports) on the NOPAT and therefore the EVA of the project would fall. These two effects are captured in Equations 11.5 and 11.6, were τ_E and τ represent the tariffs on exports and imports respectively.

$$CV_0 = W_0 + \sum_{t=1}^{\infty} f^t \left[\frac{e_t p_{I,t} \cdot q_{I,t} \cdot (1-\tau_E) - \mathbf{w}_t \mathbf{L}_t}{W_{t-1}} - c \right] W_{t-1} \quad 11.5$$

$$CV_0 = W_0 + \sum_{t=1}^{\infty} f^t \left[\frac{\mathbf{p}_t \mathbf{q}_t - e_t w_t \cdot L_t \cdot (1+\tau_I)}{W_{t-1}} - c \right] W_{t-1} \quad 11.6$$

Of course, there are other known effects from trade restrictions. As international specialization is constrained and therefore there is less scope to benefit from comparative advantages, overall efficiency (value creation) decreases. For instance, in these two equations, we assume for simplicity that all output is exported or that all inputs are imported. This, of course, is not generally the case. For instance, a tariff on importing of inputs has a direct effect on those goods. As quantity of imports fall, some industries may have to resort to local, more expensive suppliers. Our focus in this final chapter is simply to offer a general application or base guideline of institutional constraints in a simple EVA formulation.

EFW area 5: regulation

Consider now the fifth and final area which is about market regulations that restrict domestic trade. The application is straightforward. Since more regulatory requirements imply more costs, there is a fall in EVA due to the costs associated with regulatory compliance. Let $\mathcal{R}$ capture the cost of regulatory compliance. Then CV becomes Equation 11.7.

$$CV_0 = W_0 + \sum_{t=1}^{\infty} f^t \left[\frac{p_{I,t} q_{I,t} - w_t L_t - \mathcal{R}}{W_{t-1}} - c \right] W_{t-1} \qquad 11.7$$

This expression shows that regulatory costs are like a burden to economic activities. The firm needs to be able to cover extra costs that are unrelated to the production of goods and services.

There is a potential connection here with the public choice literature on this topic (unexplored here). A straightforward case is that the value of $\mathcal{R}$ can be subject to rent seeking. Policymakers may have the incentive to collect a value of up to $\mathcal{R}$ – to let the firm ignore the regulations. Another case is that of regulatory capture (Stigler, 1971). If the cost of "capturing" the regulatory agency is less than $\mathcal{R}$, then firms will try to capture the regulators to minimize the cost of $\mathcal{R}$. But the capture results in greater protection to incumbents against potential competition. Certainly, other cases can be thought of. This is just an example of a general financial representation of well-known public choice problems.

Conclusions and summary

In this final chapter we presented a very simple outline of how different institutional arrangements can affect the value of economic activities across the whole economy. Those countries whose institutions are not a burden will evidence (1) higher EVAs and also (2) higher duration.

This framework shows that the impact that institutions and policy can have on CV can occur through three different channels. First, through lower revenues, which reduce EVA, and therefore also reduce CV. Second, through higher costs, which also reduce EVA and therefore also reduce CV. The only difference between these two cases is "arithmetic," in the sense that the former reduces revenues without affecting costs and the second one increase costs

Table 11.1 Summary of EFW sub-indices impact in the EVA framework

	Revenue	*Costs*	*Discount rate*
Area 1: Size of government	X		X
Area 2: Legal system and property rights			X
Area 3: Sound money	X	X	
Area 4: Freedom to trade internationally	X	X	
Area 5: Regulation		X	

Table 11.2 Marginal effects on CV

Impact on CV	
$CV_0 = W_o + \sum_{t=1}^{\infty} f^t \left(\frac{(p_t q_t - w_t L_T) - x}{W_{t-1}} - c_t \right) W_{t-1}$	$CV_0 = W_o + \sum_{t=1}^{\infty} \frac{(ROIC_t - c_t - \rho) W_{t-1}}{(1+c+\rho)^t}$
Marginal effect	
$\frac{\partial CV_0}{\partial x} = -\sum_{t=1}^{\infty} f^t < 0$	$\frac{\partial CV_0}{\partial \rho} = -\sum_{t=1}^{\infty} W_{t-1} \frac{(1+c+\rho)+(ROIC_t - c_t - \rho)t}{(1+c+\rho)^{t+1}} < 0$

without affecting revenues. Third, through a higher discount rate. This effect, however, has a double impact on CV. On the one hand, it increases the opportunity cost of the project, which reduces the EVA. On the other hand, a higher discount rate produces lower present values and therefore also reduces CV. Since this effect takes place in a term that grows exponentially, its effect can be substantial. This aligns with the need for institutional reforms for underdeveloped countries that aspire to become high-income nations. A reduction of taxes, inflation, and regulatory costs may not be enough to achieve a high duration level and the efficiency it implies. Table 11.1 summarizes the above analysis on the EFW five sub-indices.

Finally, we can summarize these effects in two groups. The first one affects EVA (either through less revenue or more costs). The second one affects the discount rate. Let x capture the negative shock to revenue (measured in nominal terms). Let ρ capture the impact on the discount rate (measure in percent terms). Table 11.2 depicts these two marginal effects.[6]

6 Strictly speaking, $\frac{\partial CV}{\partial \rho}$ is negative unless $1 + ROIC \cdot t < (c - \rho)(t - 1)$.

Chapter 12

Concluding remarks

Capital theory appears to have two balancing sides to it. On the one hand, it is a very abstract and obscure area in economic theory. It contains semantic and theoretical riddles. It is a field that requires much work in exchange for low-value outcomes. It is absent from all economics textbooks at all education levels. It seems that nothing is to be gained by delving into the labyrinth that capital theory is. Whatever had to be said on this matter, had apparently already been said by late nineteenth- and early twentieth-century economists.

On the other hand, capital theory is embedded in all economic fields. There cannot be a production function of a firm without a theory of capital. There cannot be a study of business cycles or growth without a theory of capital to support the main equations of the model, and so on. It happens to be that one of the theories that function as the building block of the significant corpus of formal economics is also one of the more abstract yet less studied fields. We have pointed to some of the reasons this situation came to be. A semantic turn on the meaning of "capital" and the mathematical simplifications needed by formal models explains much of it. Semantics, that is, words, do matter. So do the assumptions used in formal models.

Our work shines light into the dark alleys of capital theory. Illumination requires two changes. The first one is to revisit the meaning of "capital." The second consists in applying well-known and broadly used financial concepts such as present value and duration to capital-value. These two changes are made by adopting the perspective of real economic actors in the *real world*, not the economist construct of a representative agent that iives and thinks in a formal model. Investors and entrepreneurs think in terms of present values, duration, internal rates of returns, and so on. They do not think in terms of indifference curves, or aggregate demand, and aggregate supply models. Formal models do not allow for the present value and duration calculations performed daily by real-world economic agents. Most of these models do not account for time. The only way they can deal with the problem of the period of production is by ignoring the issue.

Part II discusses the history of economic thought concerning capital theory. However, this is done to show how the concept of *duration* has been present all along, even if invisible in the eyes of capital theorists (except for Hicks). This is the reason why the book starts by presenting the main financial concepts we use (Part I). The persistence of *duration* behind the scenes in the evolution of capital theory raises some questions. In particular, why is this so? We argue that this is not a coincidence. We argue that *duration* is the concept that capital theorists have sought for years but were not able to find because of the semantic-and-assumptions trap mentioned above.

However, our finance application is not just a mental gymnastics game in the dark labyrinth of capital theory. Part III shows examples, or small roadmaps, of how the financial approach can be applied to microeconomics, macroeconomics, and institutional analysis. Three of the most critical areas in economics can be conceived as sharing the same financial foundations tying them together. A financial application to capital theory sheds light on issues such as managerial economics, Cantillon effects, business cycles, growth, and development to mention some of the examples we have used.

Part III shows that there is plenty of work to be done in this area. We hope other scholars will join our efforts.

References

Acemoglu, D., & Robinson, J.A. (2012). *Why nations fail: the origins of power, prosperity and poverty*. New York: Crown Publishers.

Barnett II, W., & Block, W.E. (2005). Professor Tullock on Austrian business cycle theory. *Advances in Austrian Economics*, 8, 431–443. https://doi.org/10.1016/S1529-2134(05)08018-X

Barnett II, W., & Block, W.E. (2006). Tyler Cowen on Austrian business cycle theory: a critique. *New Perspectives on Political Economy*, 2(2), 26–85.

Baumol, W.J. (1990). Entrepreneurship: productive, unproductive, and destructive. *Journal of Political Economy*, 98(5), 893–921.

Bierwag, G., Kaufman, G., & Toevs, A. (1983). Duration: its development and use in bond portfolio management. *Financial Analysts Journal*, 39(4), 15–35.

Birner, J. (1999). The place of the Ricardo effect in Hayek's economic research programme. *Revue d'économie Politique*, 109(6), 803–816.

Block, W.E. (2001). Yes, we have no chaff: a reply to Wagner's "Austrian cycle theory: saving the wheat while discarding the chaff." *Quarterly Journal of Austrian Economics*, 4(1), 63–73.

Boettke, P.J. (1998). Economic calculation: the Austrian contribution to political economy. *Advances in Austrian Economics*, 5, 131–158.

Boettke, P.J. (2002). Information and knowledge: austrian economics in search of its uniqueness. *The Review of Austrian Economics*, 15(4), 263–274.

Boettke, P.J., Coyne, C.J., & Newman, P. (2016). The history of a tradition: Austrian economics from 1871 to 2016. *Research in the History of Economic Thought and Methodology*, 34A, 199–243.

Boettke, P.J., & O'Donnell, K.W. (2013). The failed appropriation of F. A. Hayek by formalist economics. *Critical Review*, 25(3–4), 305–341.

Böhm-Bawerk, E. von. (1890). *Capital and interest*. London and New York: Macmillan and Co., Limited.

Böhm-Bawerk, E. von. (1896). *Karl Marx and the close of his system* (1949). New York: Augustus M. Kelley.

Borio, C., & Disyatat, P. (2011). Global imbalances and the financial crisis: link or no link? *BIS Working Papers*, (346), pp. 1–37.

Boulding. K. (1936). Time and Investment. A Reply. *Economica*, 3(12), 440–442. https://doi.org 10.2307/2549249

Braun, E. (2015). Carl Menger's contribution to capital theory. *History of Economic Ideas*, 23(1), 305–325.

Braun, E. (2017). The theory of capital as a theory of capitalism. *Journal of Institutional Economics*, 13(02), 305–325. https://doi.org/10.1017/S1744137416000394

Braun, E., Lewin, P., & Cachanosky, N. (2016). Ludwig von Mises's approach to capital as a bridge between Austrian and institutional economics. *Journal of Institutional Economics*, 12(04), 847–866. https://doi.org/10.1017/S1744137416000102

Buchanan, J.M. (1975). *The collected works of James M. Buchanan. Volume 7. The limits of liberty* (2000). Indianapolis: Liberty Fund.

Buchanan, J.M. (2015). Notes on Hayek – Miami, 15 February, 1979. *The Review of Austrian Economics*, 28(3), 257–260. https://doi.org/10.1007/s11138-015-0305-0

Buchanan, J.M., & Brennan, G. (1985). *The collected works of James M. Buchanan. Volume 10. The reason of rules* (2000). Indianapolis: Liberty Fund.

Caballero, R.J. (2010). Macroeconomics after the crisis: time to deal with the pretense-of-knowledge syndrome. *Journal of Economic Perspectives*, 24(4), 85–102. https://doi.org/10.1257/jep.24.4.85

Cachanosky, J.C. (1984). La escuela austriaca de economía [The Austrian school of economics] *Libertas*, 1(Octubre).

Cachanosky, J.C. (1994). Historia de las teorías del valor y del precio I [History of theories of value and price I]. *Libertas*, 20(Mayo).

Cachanosky, J.C. (1995). Historia de las teorías del valor y el precio II [History of theories of value and price II]. *Libertas*, 22(Mayo).

Cachanosky, J.C. (1999). Value based management. *Libertas*, 30(mayo), 179–211.

Cachanosky, N. (2012). Una introducción a la economía clásica [An introduction to classical economics]. In A. Ravier (Ed.), *Lecturas de historia del pensamiento económico* (pp. 147–166). Madrid: Union Editorial.

Cachanosky, N. (2014a). The effects of U.S. monetary policy on Colombia and Panama (2002–2007). *The Quarterly Review of Economics and Finance*, 54, 428–436. https://doi.org/10.1016/j.qref.2014.03.003

Cachanosky, N. (2014b). The Mises-Hayek business cycle theory, fiat currencies and open economies. *The Review of Austrian Economics*, 27(3), 281–299. https://doi.org/10.1007/s11138-012-0188-2

Cachanosky, N. (2015a). Expectation in Austrian business cycle theory: market share matters. *The Review of Austrian Economics*, 28(2), 151–165. https://doi.org/10.1007/s11138-014-0267-7

Cachanosky, N. (2015b). U.S. monetary policy's impact on Latin America's structure of production (1960–2010). *Latin American Journal of Economics*, 51(2), 95–116. https://doi.org/10.7764/LAJE.52.1.95

Cachanosky, N., & Hoffmann, A. (2016). Monetary policy, the composition of GDP and crisis duration in Europe. *Global Economic Review*, 45(2), 206–219. https://doi.org/10.1080/1226508X.2015.1137484

Cachanosky, N., & Lewin, P. (2014). Roundaboutness is not a mysterious concept: a financial application to capital theory. *Review of Political Economy*, 26(4), 648–665. https://doi.org/10.1080/09538259.2014.957475

Cachanosky, N., & Lewin, P. (2016a). An empirical application of the EVA® framework to business cycles. *Review of Financial Economics*, 30(September), 60–67. https://doi.org/10.1016/j.rfe.2016.06.006

Cachanosky, N., & Lewin, P. (2016b). Financial foundations of Austrian business cycle theory. *Advances in Austrian Economics*, 20, 15–44. https://doi.org/10.1108/S1529-213420160000020002

Cachanosky, N., & Padilla, A. (2017). Economic and philosophical implications of Hayek's knowledge problem. *Libertas: Segunda Epoca*, 2(1), 67–79.

Cachanosky, N., & Salter, A.W. (2017). The view from Vienna: an analysis of the renewed interest in the Mises-Hayek theory of the business cycle. *The Review of Austrian Economics*, 30(2), 169–192. https://doi.org/10.1007/s11138-016-0340-5

Caldwell, B.J. (1984). Some problems with falsification in economics. *Philosophy of the Social Sciences*, 14, 489–495.

Caldwell, B.J. (1997). Hayek and socialism. *Journal of Economic Literature*, 35(4), 1856–1890.

Callahan, G., & Horwitz, S.G. (2010). The role of ideal types in Austrian business cycle theory. *Advances in Austrian Economics*, 14, 205–224. https://doi.org/10.1108/S1529-2134(2010) 0000014013

Calvo, G.A. (2013). Puzzling over the anatomy of crises: liquidity and the veil of finance. *Monetary and Economic Studies*, (November), 39–63.

Caplan, B. (1997). *Why I am not an Austrian economist*. Unpublished Manuscript. Retrieved from http://econfaculty.gmu.edu/bcaplan/whyaust.htm

Carilli, A.M., & Dempster, G.M. (2001). Expectations in Austrian business cycle theory: an application of the prisoner's dilemma. *The Review of Austrian Economics*, 14(4), 319–330.

Coase, R.H. (1973). Business organization and the accountant. In L.*S.E. Essays on Cost*. London: Weidenfeld and Nicolson.

Cohen, A.J. (2008). The mythology of capital or of static equilibrium? The Böhm-Bawerk/Clark controversy. *Journal of the History of Economic Thought*, 30(02), 151–171. https://doi.org/10.1017/S1042771608000161

Cohen, A.J. (2010). Capital controversy from Böhm-Bawerk to Bliss: badly posed or very deep questions? or what "we" can learn from capital controversy even if we don't care who won. *Journal of the History of Economic Thought*, 32(01), 1–21. https://doi.org/10.1017/S105383720999040X

Cohen, A.J., & Harcourt, G.C. (2003). Whatever happened to the Cambridge capital theory controversies? Preliminaries: Joan Robinson's complaints. *Journal of Economic Perspectives*, 17(1), 199–214.

Cowen, T. (1997). *Risk and business cycles: new and old Austrian perspectives*. New York: Routledge.

Coyne, C.J. (2008). *After war: the political economy of exporting democracy*. Stanford: Stanford Economics and Finance.

Coyne, C.J., Leeson, P.T., & Boettke, P.J. (2005). Hayek vs. the neoclassicists: lessons from the socialist calculation debate. In *Elgar Companion to Hayekian Economics*. Edward Elgar Publishing.

Diamond, D.W., & Rajan, R.G. (2009). The credit crisis: conjectures about causes and remedies. *American Economic Review*, 99(2), 606–610. https://doi.org/10.1257/aer.99.2.606

Diamond, D.W., & Rajan, R.G. (2012). Illiquid banks, financial stability, and interest rate policy. *Journal of Political Economy*, 120(3), 552–591.

Dixit, A.K. (2009). Governance institutions and economic activity. *American Economic Review*, 99(1), 5–24. https://doi.org/10.1257/aer.99.1.5

Dixit, A.K., & Pyndick, R.S. (1994). *Irreversible investment*. Princeton: Princeton University Press.

Dorfman, R. (1959a). A graphical exposition of Böhm-Bawerk's interest theory. The *Review of Economic Studies*, 26(2), 153–158.

Dorfman, R. (1959b). Waiting and the period of production. *Quarterly Journal of Economics*, 73(3), 351–372.

Easterly, W. (2008). Institutions: top down or bottom up? *American Economic Review*, 98(2), 95–99. https://doi.org/10.1257/aer.98.2.95

Ehrbar, A. (1998). *EVA: the real key to creating wealth*. Hoboken: Wiley Publishers.

Eusepi, S., & Preston, B. (2011). Expectations, learning, and business cycle fluctuations. *American Economic Review*, 101(6), 2844–2872. https://doi.org/10.1257/aer.101.6.2844

Evans, A.J., Baxendale, T. (2008). Austrian business cycle theory in light of rational expectations: the role of heterogeneity, the monetary footprint, and adverse selection in monetary expansion. *The Quarterly Journal of Austrian Economics*, 11(2), 81), 81–93. https://doi.org/10.1007/s12113-008-9034-6

Faber, M. (1979). *An introduction to modern Austrian capital theory*. New York: Verlag.

Felipe, J., & Fisher, F.M. (2006). Aggregate production functions, neoclassical growth models and the aggregation problem. *Estudios de Economica Applicada*, 24(1), 127–163.

Felipe, J., & McCombie, J.S.L. (2014). The aggregate production function: 'not even wrong.' *Review of Political Economy*, 26(1), 60–84. https://doi.org/10.1080/09538259.2013.874192

Fetter, F.A. (1977). *Capital, interest and rent*. Kansas City: Sheed Andrews and McMeel.

Fisher, F.M. (2005). Aggregate production functions – a pervasive but unpersuasive fairytale. *Eastern Economic Journal*, 31(3), 489–491.

Fisher, F.M., & Monz, J. (1993). *Aggregation: aggregate production functions and related topics* (1st MIT Pr). Cambridge, Mass: MIT Press.

Fisher, I. (1906). *The nature of capital and income*. London: MacMillan.

Fisher, I. (1933). The debt-deflation theory of the great depression. Econometrica, 1(4), 337–359.

Friedman, M., & Schwartz, A.J. (1963). Money and business cycles. *The Review of Economics and Statistics*, 45(1), 32–64.

Fuster, A., Laibson, D., & Mendel, B. (2010). Natural expectations and macroeconomic fluctuations. *Journal of Economic Perspectives*, 24(4), 67–84.

Garrison, R.W. (1986). From Lachmann to Lucas: on institutions, expectations, and equilibrating tendencies. In I.M. Kirzner (Ed.), *Subjectivism, Intelligibility and Economic Understanding* (pp. 87–101). New York and London: New York University Press and Macmillan Co.

Garrison, R W. (2001). *Time and money. the macroeconomics of capital structure*. (2002). London and New York: Routledge.

Gwartney, J., Holcombe, R.G., & Lawson, R.A. (2004). Economic freedom, institutional quality, and cross-country-differences in income and growth. *Cato Journal*, 24(3), 205–233.

Gwartney, J., Lawson, R.A., Hall, J., & Murphy, R.H. (2018). *Economic freedom of the world: 2018 annual report*. Fraser Institute.

Hall, J.C., & Lawson, R.A. (2014). Economic freedom of the world: an accounting of the literature. *Contemporary Economic Policy*, 32(1), 1–19. https://doi.org/10.1111/coep.12010

Hayek, F.A. (1931). *Prices and oroduction* (1967). New York: Augustus M. Kelley.
Hayek, F.A. (1933). *Monetary theory and the trade cycle*. New York: Sentry Press.
Hayek, F.A. (1934). On the relationship between investment and output. *The Economic Journal*, 44(174), 207–231.
Hayek, F.A. (1935). The maintenance of capital. *Economica*, 2(7), 241–276.
Hayek, F.A. (1936). The mythology of capital. *The Quarterly Journal of Economics*, 50(2), 199–228.
Hayek, F.A. (1941). *The pure theory of capital*. (2007). Chicago: Chicago University Press.
Hayek, F.A. (1948). *Individualism and economic order* (1958). Chicago: The University of Chicago Press.
Hayek, F.A. (1973). *Law, legislation and liberty: rules and order. Volume 1*. (1983). Chicago: The University of Chicago Press.
Hayek, F.A. (1976). *Law, legislation and liberty: the mirage of social justice. Volume 2*. (1978). Chicago: The University of Chicago Press.
Hayek, F.A. (1979). *Law, legislation and liberty: the political order of a free people. Volume 3*. (1981). Chicago: The University of Chicago Press.
Hayek, F.A. (1984). *Money, capital, and fluctuations: early essays*. Chicago: The University of Chicago Press.
Hendrickson, J.R. (2017). Interest rates and investment coordination failures. *The Review of Austrian Economics*, 30(4), 493–515. https://doi.org/10.1007/s11138-016-0368-6
Hendrickson, J.R., & Salter, A.W. (2016). Money, liquidity, and the structure of production. *Journal of Economic Dynamics and Control*, 73, 314–328. https://doi.org/10.1016/j.jedc.2016.10.001
Hicks, J.R. (1939). *Value and capital* (2001). Oxford: Oxford University Press.
Hicks, J.R. (1965). *Capital and growth*. Oxford: Oxford University Press.
Hicks, J.R. (1973a). *Capital and time*. Oxford: Oxford University Press.
Hicks, J.R. (1973b). The Austrian theory of capital and its rebirth in modern economics. In *Carl Menger and the Austrian School of Economics*. Oxford: Clarendon Press.
Hicks, J.R. (1976). Some questions of time in economics. In *Evolution, welfare and time in economics, Festschrift in honor of Nicholas Georgescu-Roegenr*. Lexington: Lexington Books.
Hicks, J.R. (1979). Is interest rate the price of a factor of production? In M.J. Rizzo (Ed.), *Time, uncertainty, and disequilibrium: exploration in Austrian themes*. Lexington, Toronto: Lexington Books.
Higgs, R. (2009). Regime uncertainty. *The Independent Review*, 1(4), 561–590.
Hodgson, G.M. (2014). What is capital? Economists and sociologists have changed its meaning: should it be changed back? *Cambridge Journal of Economics*, 38(5), 1063–1086. https://doi.org/10.1093/cje/beu013
Hoffmann, A. (2010). An overinvestment cycle in Central and Eastern Europe? *Metroeconomica*, 61(4), 711–734. https://doi.org/10.1111/j.1467-999X.2010.04103.x
Hoffmann, A., & Cachanosky, N. (2018). Unintended consequences of ECB policies in Europe. In A. Kroon, Godart van-der & P. Vonlanthen (Eds.), *Banking and monetary policy from the perspective of Austrian economics* (pp. 103–126). Cham: Springer International Publishing. https://doi.org/10.1007/978-3-319-75817-6_6
Hoffmann, A., & Schnabl, G. (2011). A vicious cycle of manias, crises and asymmetric policy responses – an overinvestment view. *The world economy*, 34(3), 382–403. https://doi.org/10.1111/j.1467-9701.2011.01334.x

Horwitz, S. (2011). Contrasting concepts of capital: yet another look at the Hayek-Keynes debate. *Journal of Private Enterprise*, 27(1), 9–27.

Hume, M., & Sentance, A. (2009). The global credit boom: challenges for macroeconomics and policy. *Journal of International Money and Finance*, 28(8), 1426–1461. https://doi.org/10.1016/j.jimonfin.2009.08.009

Jaffé, W. (1976). Menger, Jevons and Walras de-homogenized. *Economic Inquiry*, 14(4), 511–524. https://doi.org/10.1111/j.1465-7295.1976.tb00439.x

Jevons, W.S. (1871). *The theory of political economy* (1888). London and New York: Macmillan and Co., Limited.

Kirzner, I.M. (1960). *The economic point of view*. (1976). Kansas City: Sheed and Ward, Inc.

Kirzner, I.M. (1996[2010]). *Essays on capital and interest*. Indianapolis: Liberty Fund.

Kirzner, I.M. (2000). *The driving force of the market*. London and New York: Routledge.

Kirzner, I.M. (2010). *Essays on capital and interest*. Indianapolis: Liberty Fund.

Knight, F.H. (1935). Professor Hayek and the theory of investment. *The Economic Journal*, 45(177), 77–94.

Koller, T., Goedhart, M., & Wessels, D. (1990). *Valuation: measuring and managing the value of companies* (2010). Hoboken: Wiley.

Koppl, R.G. (2014). *From crisis to confidence: macroeconomics after the crash*. London: Institute of Economic Affairs.

Lachmann, L.M. (1940). A reconsideration of the Austrian theory of industrial fluctuations. *Economica*, (May), 179–196.

Lachmann, L.M. (1947). Complementarity and substitution in the theory of capital. *Economica*, 14, 108–119.

Lachmann, L.M. (1948). Investment repercussions. The Quarterly Journal of Economics, 62(5), 698–713.

Lachmann, L.M. (1956). *Capital and its structure*. Kansas City: Sheed Andrews and McMeel.

Lachmann, L.M. (1986). *The market as an economic process*. Oxford, UK ; New York, NY, USA: B. Blackwell.

Leijonhufvud, A. (2009). Out of the corridor: Keynes and the crisis. *Cambridge Journal of Economics*, 33(4), 741–757. https://doi.org/10.1093/cje/bep022

Lester, R.B., & Wolff, J.S. (2013). The empirical relevance of the Mises-Hayek theory of the trade cycle. *The Review of Austrian Economics*, 26(4), 433–461. https://doi.org/10.1007/s11138-013-0225-9

Lewin, P. (1997). Capital and time: variations on a Hicksian theme. *Advances in Austrian Economics*, 4, 63–74.

Lewin, P. (1998). The firm, money, and economic calculation: considering the institutional nexus of market production. *American Journal of Economics and Sociology*, 57(4), 499–512. https://doi.org/10.1111/j.1536-7150.1998.tb03378.x

Lewin, P. (1999). *Capital in disequilibrium* (2011). Auburn: Ludwig von Mises Institute.

Lewin, P. (2018). The microfoundations of the microfoundations of Austrian business cycle theory. *The Review of Austrian Economics*. https://doi.org/10.1007/s11138-018-0430-7

Lewin, P., & Cachanosky, N. (2016). A financial framework for understanding macroeconomic cycles. *Journal of Financial Economic Policy*, 8(2), 268–280. https://doi.org/10.1108/JFEP-07-2015-0041

Lewin, P., & Cachanosky, N. (2018). The average period of production: the history and rehabilitation of an idea. *Journal of the History of Economic Thought*, 40(1), 81–98. https://doi.org/10.1017/S105383721700013X

Lewin, P., & Cachanosky, N. (2019). *Austrian capital theory: a modern survey of the essentials*. Cambridge: Cambridge University Press.

Lucas, R.E. (1972). Expectations and the neutrality of money. *Journal of Economic Theory*, 4(2), 103–124.

Lucas, R.E. (1973). Some international evidence on output-inflation tradeoffs. *The American Economic Review*, 63(3), 326–334.

Lucas, R.E. (1975). An equilibrium model of the business cycle. *Journal of Political Economy*, 83(6), 1113–1144. https://doi.org/10.1086/260386

Luther, W.J., & Cohen, M. (2014). An empirical analysis of the Austrian business cycle theory. *Atlantic Economic Journal*, 42(2), 153–169. https://doi.org/10.1007/s11293-014-9415-5

Lutz, F. (1967). *The theory of interest*. Dordrech: Reidel Publishing Company.

Macaulay, F.R. (1938). *The movements of interest rates. Bond yields and stock prices in the United States since 1856*. New York: National Bureau of Economic Research.

Machlup, F. (1935a). The "period of production": a further word. *The Journal of Political Economy*, 43(6), 808.

Machlup, F. (1935b). Professor knight and the period of production. *The Journal of Political Economy*, 43(5), 577–624.

Machlup, F. (1955). The problem of verification in economics. *Southern Economic Journal*, 22(1), 1–21.

McClure, J., Spector, L., & Thomas, D. (2018). Hayek's tacit knowledge. *SSRN Electronic Journal*. https://doi.org/10.2139/ssrn.3213973

Menger, C. (1871). *Principles of economics* (2004). Auburn: The Ludwig von Mises Institute.

Menger, C. (1892). On the origins of money. *The Economic Journal*, 2, 239–255.

Mises, L. von. (1912). *The theory of money and credit*. (1981). Indianapolis: Liberty Fund.

Mises, L. von. (1920). Economic calculation in the socialist commonwealth. *Archiv für Sozialwissenschaften*, 47.

Mises, L. von. (1922). *Socialism*. (1962). New Haven: Yale University Press.

Mises, L. von. (1933). *Epistemological problems of economics* (2003). Auburn: The Ludwig von Mises Institute.

Mises, L. von. (1943). "Elastic expectations" and the Austrian theory of the trade cycle. *Economica*, 10(39), 251–252.

Mises, L. von. (1949). *Human action* (1996). Irvington-on-Hudson: The Foundation for Economic Education.

Mises, L. von. (1969). *Historical setting of the Austrian school of economics* (2003). Auburn: Ludwig von Mises Institute.

Mulligan, R.F. (2002). A Hayekian analysis of the structure of production. *Quarterly Journal of Austrian Economics*, 5(2), 17–33.

Murphy, R.P. (2015). *Choice: cooperation, enterprise, and human action*. Oakland, CA: Independent Institute.

North, D. (1991). Institutions. *Journal of Economic Perspectives*, 5(1), 97–112.

O'Driscoll, G.P.J., & Rizzo, M.J. (1985). *The economics of time and ignorance*. (1996). New York: Routledge.

Olson, M. (2000). *Power and prosperity*. New York: Basic Books.

Osborne, M. (2005). On the computation of a formula for the duration of a bond that yields precise results. *Quarterly Review of Economics and Finance*, 45(1), 161–183.

Osborne, M. (2014). *Multiple interest rate analysis*. Houndsmill, Basingstoke: Palgrave.

Osborne, M., & Davidson, I. (2016). The Cambridge capital controversies: contributions from the complex plane. *Review of Political Economy*, 28(2), 251–269. https://doi.org/10.1080/09538259.2015.1129751

Ostrom, E. (2010). Beyond markets and states: polycentric governance of complex economic systems. *American Economic Review*, 100(3), 641–672. https://doi.org/10.1257/aer.100.3.641

Padilla, A., & Cachanosky, N. (2016). Indirectly productive entrepreneurship. *Journal of Entrepreneurship and Public Policy*, 5(2), 161–175. https://doi.org/10.1108/JEPP-03-2015-0016

Pigou, A. (1935). Net income and capital depletion. *Economic Journal*, 45(178), 235–241.

Pigou, A. (1941). Maintaining capital intact. *Economica*, 8(31), 271–273.

Pigou, A.C. (1932). *The economics of welfare* (2017). London New York: Routledge.

Powell, B.W. (2002). Explaining Japan's recession. *The Quarterly Journal of Austrian Economics*, 5(2), 35–50.

Redington, F.M. (1952). Review of the principles of life-office valuations. *Journal of the Institute of Actuaries*, 78(3), 286–315.

Ricardo, D. (1891). *On the principles of political economy and taxation*. London: G. Bell and sons.

Robbins, L. (1934). *The Great Depression* (1971). Freeport, New York: Books for Libraries Press.

Salter, A.W., & Luther, W.J. (2016). The optimal Austrian business cycle theory. *Advances in Austrian Economics*, 20, 45–60. https://doi.org/10.1108/S1529-213420160000020003

Schumpeter, J.A. (1942). *Capitalism, socialism and democracy* (2010). London: George Allen and Unwin.

Scott, M. (1984). Maintaining capital intact. *Oxford Economic Papers*, 36(Nov.), 59–73.

Smith, A. (1776). *An inquiry into the nature and causes of the wealth of nations*. (1979). Indianapolis: Liberty Classics.

Solow, R. (1956). A contribution to the theory of economic growth. *Quarterly Journal of Economics*, 70(1), 65–94.

Stern, J.M., Shiely, J.S., & Ross, I. (2003). *The EVA challenge*. New York: Wiley.

Stigler, G.J. (1971). The theory of economic regulation. *The Bell Journal of Economics and Management Science*, 2(1), 3–21. https://doi.org/10.2307/3003160

Swan, T. (1956). Economic growth and capital accumulation. *Economic Record*, 32(2), 334–361.

Tullock, G. (1988). Why the Austrians are wrong about depressions. *The Review of Austrian Economics*, 2(1), 73–78.

Tullock, G. (1989). Reply to comment by Joseph T. Salerno. *The Review of Austrian Economics*, 3(1), 147–149.

Uhr, C. (1960). *Economic doctrines of Knut Wicksell*. Berkely and Los Angeles: University of California Press.

Wagner, R.E. (1999). Austrian cycle theory: saving the wheat while discarding the chaff. *The Review of Austrian Economics*, 12, 65–80.

White, L.H. (1941). Introduction. In *The pure theory of capital* (2007). Chicago: Chicago University Press.

Williamson, C. (2009). Informal institutions rule: institutional arrangements and economic performance. *Public Choice*, 139(3), 371–387.

Young, A.T. (2005). Reallocating labor to initiate changes in capital structures: Hayek revisited. *Economics Letters*, 89(3), 275–282. https://doi.org/10.1016/j.econlet.2005.05.033

Young, A.T. (2012). The time structure of production in the US, 2002–2009. *The Review of Austrian Economics*, 25(2), 77–92. https://doi.org/10.1007/s11138-011-0158-0

Young, A.T. (2015). Austrian business cycle theory: a modern appraisal. In P.J. Boettke & C.J. Coyne (Eds.), *Oxford handbook of Austrian economics*. Oxford: Oxford University Press.

Young, D.S., & O'Byrne, S.E. (2000). *EVA and value-based management*. New York: McGraw-Hill.

Zanotti, G.J., & Cachanosky, N. (2015). Implications of Machlup's interpretation of Mises's epistemology. *Journal of the History of Economic Thought*, 37(01), 111–138. https://doi.org/10.1017/S1053837214000777

Index